The Cambridge Introduction to
Emily Dickinson

Emily Dickinson is best known as an intensely private, even reclusive writer. Yet the way she has been mythologized has meant her work is often misunderstood. This introduction delves behind the myth to present a poet who was deeply engaged with the issues of her day. In a lucid and elegant style, the book places her life and work in the historical context of the Civil War, the suffrage movement, and the rapid industrialization of the United States. Wendy Martin explores the ways in which Dickinson's personal struggles with romantic love, religious faith, friendship, and community shape her poetry. The complex publication history of her works, as well as their reception, is teased out, and a guide to further reading is included. Dickinson emerges not only as one of America's finest poets, but also as a fiercely independent intellect and an original talent writing poetry far ahead of her time.

Wendy Martin is Professor of American Literature and American Studies at Claremont Graduate University and the editor of *The Cambridge Companion to Emily Dickinson* (2002).

Cambridge Introductions to Literature

This series is designed to introduce students to key topics and authors. Accessible and lively, these introductions will also appeal to readers who want to broaden their understanding of the books and authors they enjoy.

- Ideal for students, teachers, and lecturers
- Concise, yet packed with essential information
- Key suggestions for further reading

Titles in this series:

Eric Bulson *The Cambridge Introduction to James Joyce*

John Xiros Cooper *The Cambridge Introduction to T. S. Eliot*

Kirk Curnutt *The Cambridge Introduction to F. Scott Fitzgerald*

Janette Dillon *The Cambridge Introduction to Early English Theatre*

Janette Dillon *The Cambridge Introduction to Shakespeare's Tragedies*

Jane Goldman *The Cambridge Introduction to Virginia Woolf*

Kevin J. Hayes *The Cambridge Introduction to Herman Melville*

David Holdeman *The Cambridge Introduction to W. B. Yeats*

M. Jimmie Killingsworth *The Cambridge Introduction to Walt Whitman*

Rónán McDonald *The Cambridge Introduction to Samuel Beckett*

Wendy Martin *The Cambridge Introduction to Emily Dickinson*

Peter Messent *The Cambridge Introduction to Mark Twain*

John Peters *The Cambridge Introduction to Joseph Conrad*

Sarah Robbins *The Cambridge Introduction to Harriet Beecher Stowe*

Martin Scofield *The Cambridge Introduction to the American Short Story*

Emma Smith *The Cambridge Introduction to Shakespeare*

Peter Thomson *The Cambridge Introduction to English Theatre, 1660–1900*

Janet Todd *The Cambridge Introduction to Jane Austen*

Jennifer Wallace *The Cambridge Introduction to Tragedy*

The Cambridge Introduction to
Emily Dickinson

WENDY MARTIN

CAMBRIDGE
UNIVERSITY PRESS

811.4
D55zmara

CAMBRIDGE UNIVERSITY PRESS
Cambridge, New York, Melbourne, Madrid, Cape Town, Singapore, São Paulo

Cambridge University Press
The Edinburgh Building, Cambridge CB2 2RU, UK

Published in the United States of America by Cambridge University Press, New York

www.cambridge.org
Information on this title: www.cambridge.org/9780521672702

First published 2007

Printed in the United Kingdom at the University Press, Cambridge

A catalogue record for this publication is available from the British Library

Library of Congress Cataloguing in Publication data

Martin, Wendy, 1940–
The Cambridge introduction to Emily Dickinson / by Wendy Martin.
    p.   cm. – (Cambridge introductions to literature)
Includes bibliographical references and index.
ISBN-13: 978-0-521-85670-6
ISBN-10: 0-521-85670-1
ISBN-13: 978-0-521-67270-2 (pbk.)
ISBN-13: 0-521-67270-8 (pbk.)
1. Dickinson, Emily, 1830–1886 – Criticism and interpretation.   I. Title.
II. Series.
PS1541 . Z5M37   2007

811'.4 – dc22
2006032442

ISBN 978-0-521-85670-6 hardback
ISBN 978-0-521-67270-2 paperback

Contents

Preface   *page* vii
Acknowledgments   x

Chapter 1 Life   1

The Dickinson family   1
A portrait of the poet as a young girl   5
Early ambitions, difficult changes   10
Preceptors   14
"Sister Sue"   15
A "Woman – white – to be"   18

Chapter 2 Context   24

Religious culture: Puritanism, the Great
     Awakenings, and revivals   24
Industrialization and the individual   27
Political culture: expansion and the antebellum
     period   28
Social movements: Abolition and women's
     rights   30
Philosophical reactions: Transcendentalism   32
The Civil War   34

Chapter 3 Works   40

Sweeping with many-colored brooms: the
     influence of the domestic   51
Blasphemous devotion: biblical allusion in the
     poems and letters   58

"Easy, quite, to love": friendship and love in
    Dickinson's life and works   70
"The Heaven – below": nature poems   86
"A Riddle, at the last": death and immortality 97

Chapter 4 Reception   110

"The Auction Of the Mind": publication
    history   110
Editing the poems and letters   117
Early reception   121
New Criticism   123
Dickinson's legacy today   128

Notes   132
Guide to further reading   139
Index   144

Preface

Emily Dickinson (1830–86) was a deceptively quiet nineteenth-century American woman who wrote with the fire, innovation, and skill of a twentieth-century master. Long before the Modernist and feminist movements, Dickinson wrote astonishingly prescient poetry that embodied principles of fragmentation, isolation, independence, and self-reliance. The "half-cracked poetess" and "Belle of Amherst" was misunderstood and mythologized in life and in death, leaving a trail of editors, readers, and scholars perplexed by her idiosyncratic use of meter, rhyme, capitalization, and punctuation.

Dickinson dared to live according to her own rules rather than by conventional social codes and carved a space for herself in a period that allowed women very little room. Often misunderstood as a victim of Victorian culture, Dickinson deliberately worked within cultural constraints, often assuming an ironic and playful stance toward conventional values while finding American individualism, self, and voice through her poetry and letters.

This book is an introduction to the woman behind the myth, to the life, letters, and poetry of one of America's most cherished artists. It is divided into four main chapters: Life, Context, Works, and Reception.

The first chapter of the book provides a portrait of Dickinson's life, from her childhood in Amherst to her momentous decision to retreat from the world and focus on the art of poetry. As a precocious girl, Dickinson loved books, nature, friends, and school. She grew up in a narrow, provincial town where anyone who did not follow the status quo was vilified. Despite rigid instruction from teachers, society, religion, and her own demanding father, the young Dickinson began to break away from society's expectations and forge her own distinct place in the world. This chapter describes the family that influenced Emily Dickinson, the homes where she spent her childhood and adulthood, and her life at school and college. It also describes her intense friendships and relationships, including the women she corresponded with for decades and the male "Preceptors" who had a powerful impact upon her writing. Knowledge of Dickinson's biography helps the reader understand the life events and personal motivations that influenced her extraordinary letters and poetry.

The second chapter of this book examines Dickinson as a Civil War poet and places her in the context of cultural and historical events. On the surface, Dickinson's writings may suggest a naïve ignorance of the sweeping changes taking place in nineteenth-century New England, but Dickinson's investment in this world and this life meant that she was keenly aware and deeply interested in the shaping influences of industrialization, the Abolition and women's rights movements, Transcendentalism, and the Civil War. While Dickinson was never a public figure engaged in political movements, their consequences and ramifications could not fail to affect her. Dickinson's poetry and letters explore the ideas behind these movements on a personal level; her poetry captures the struggle between independence and subjection that is very much at the heart of the Civil War and the women's rights movements. Her internal conflicts between self-determination and obedience to alien social and religious codes – to master herself or be mastered by others – mirror the larger political and social issues of her day.

Discussions about the rights of the individual soul, about independence and autonomy that were crucial to the Abolition and women's rights movements were also crucial to Dickinson; her poetry is a nuanced and profoundly personal chronicle of the larger social struggle in regard to selfhood and submission. Likewise, Dickinson's love for nature is informed by and responds to Transcendentalism and Industrialization, but again in a deeply personal way. This chapter of the book links Dickinson to the momentous social, political and economic challenges and crises through which she lived.

The third and longest chapter of the book deals with the body of Dickinson's writing, including discussions of her poetry and letters. It provides an introduction to Dickinson's unique worldview and poetic style. This chapter also discusses the ways her work maps the soul and records the experience of each moment. It moves on to discuss Dickinson's use of domestic images in her poetry and her use of the Bible to describe her devotion, not to God, but to her loved ones and to nature. Dickinson found both ecstasy and devastation in her relationships with others, and she recorded these feelings in her work. She felt a similar connection to nature – its beauty as well as terrors. These themes – love, friendship, and nature – constantly reappear in Dickinson's work and are treated in separate sections within the chapter.

Of course, the darkest aspect of nature and a theme around which Dickinson wrote some of her greatest poetry is the problem of death, which is accorded a separate section of its own. Intrigued by its mystery and inevitability, Dickinson was determined to fully explore the concept of death and to experience the emotions it aroused to their fullest extent. Dickinson's acceptance of death allowed her to treasure life in all its complexity.

The book's final chapter explores the complex and controversial publication history of Dickinson's manuscripts and how they have been received by critics and scholars over the last 150 years, tracing Dickinson's movement from an obscure and unknown poet to one of the most popular and influential poets in American history.

Finally, the Guide to Further Reading provides an annotated list of the most important and helpful resources for beginning a study of this great American poet.

Note and abbreviations

L followed by page and letter number: Thomas H. Johnson (ed.), *The Letters of Emily Dickinson* (Cambridge: Harvard University Press, 1986)

P followed by page and poem number: Thomas H. Johnson (ed.), *The Complete Poems of Emily Dickinson* (New York: Little, Brown and Company, 1960)

Dickinson's original spellings, punctuation, and capitalization have been retained. *Sic* has been omitted throughout this book.

Acknowledgments

I would like to thank Claremont Graduate University graduate students Jeffrey Morano, Mary Powell, and Tara Prescott for their substantial and important contributions to this book. They enthusiastically participated in every phase of this project, from research and writing to analysis and editing. I am especially grateful to Mary Powell for her insightful work on the Works chapter, "Blasphemous devotion: biblical allusion in the poems and letters," "'Easy, quite, to love': friendship and love in Dickinson's life and works," "'The Heaven – below': nature poems," and "'A Riddle, at the last': death and immortality" and to Tara Prescott for her work on the Life, Context, and Reception chapters, as well as "Sweeping with many-colored brooms: the influence of the domestic," in the Works chapter. Thank you also to the students of Claremont Graduate University's Fall 2005 Emily Dickinson Seminar, with special thanks to Teresa Boyer, Jessica Groper, and Joshua Jensen.

Chapter 1

Life

The Dickinson family *2*
A portrait of the poet as a young girl *5*
Early ambitions, difficult changes *10*
Preceptors *14*
"Sister Sue" *15*
A "Woman – white – to be" *18*

The shore is safer, Abiah, but I love to buffet the sea – I can count the
bitter wrecks here in these pleasant waters, and hear the murmuring
winds, but oh, I love the danger!
> Emily Dickinson, letter to Abiah Root, 1850; *L* 104, no. 39

Emily Dickinson was wickedly funny, fiercely loyal, and bravely original. She
was a poet before her time, an under-appreciated writer who experimented
with poetry and stretched the limits of an unmarried woman's role long before
the Modernist and feminist movements of the twentieth century. Although
many historians have tried to label her, Dickinson's unusual life and original
poetry defy easy categorization. Readers approaching her work for the first time
are often surprised. Dickinson lived and wrote more than a hundred years ago,
yet readers can identify with her as if she were living next door today. Although
she knew "the shore is safer," Emily Dickinson threw her life and work into
navigating the terrifying aspects of life and death, charting "the danger" for
future generations.

Dickinson was a model for all women poets who followed – an example of
eccentricity, autonomy, and rebellion. She lived in a society where women were
generally expected to be dutiful rather than creative or productive, models of
decorum rather than innovators, and above all wives and mothers. The time,
the culture, and the odds were stacked against an intellectual, literary woman.
Yet, Emily Dickinson used the resources of her family, home, and network of
friends to shatter the narrow role society offered her and become one of the
most influential American poets.

The Dickinson family

Emily Dickinson was born in Amherst, Massachusetts, a small New England town where everyone knew everyone else's business. News traveled quickly by word of mouth at community gatherings, church services, funerals, and social visits, when people would "call upon" neighbors and friends. Dickinson and her neighbors knew intimate details about each other, including everything from who purchased a new calico or was wearing the latest fashion in hats to who was having a baby or an affair. Gossip spread through a tightly woven web of conversations and letters. In the following letter, the fourteen-year-old Dickinson demonstrates the gossipy nature of a teenager living in a very small, inter-connected town:

> I do not understand your hints in regard to Abby taking so much interest in Deacon Macks family. Now Sarah is absent, I take it William is the member of the family whom you allude to. But I did not know as Abby had any partiality for him. That William is a smart boy. However as you did not mean to insinuate I will make no more comments on him, except to add that I think he will make a devoted *husband*. Dont you. I am sorry that you are laying up Hattys sins against her. I think you had better heap coals of fire upon her head by writing to her constantly until you get an answer . . . I dont know about this Mr Eastcott giving you concert tickets. I think for my part it looks rather suspicious. He is a young man I suppose. These Music teachers are always such high souled beings that I think they would exactly suit your fancy.   (*L* 17–18, no. 7)

Her ability to jump from Abby to Sarah, William, Hatty, and Mr Eastcott demonstrates an ease and familiarity with discussing the personal details of multiple people. In fact, crushes ("partiality for him"), suitability for marriage ("he will make a devoted *husband*"), and unusual behavior ("it looks rather suspicious") were cause for plenty of gossip in Amherst. Dickinson herself had many crushes, never married, and exhibited very unusual behavior for her time. This may be why myths that were created about her have been perpetuated until the present day.

The Dickinson family name was well known and established long before Emily Dickinson's birth. Her paternal grandfather, Samuel, helped found Amherst College and funded various projects within town. When Emily Dickinson's father, Edward, was born, the family name was associated with wealth and social prominence. However, Samuel Dickinson funded schemes that were not financially viable, spent money his family could not afford to lose, and ultimately caused their financial ruin.

Edward Dickinson was forced to live on a shoestring budget at school, often sacrificing necessities that his classmates took for granted. His family's relentless financial struggles and the responsibility and shame for his father's mistakes forced Edward Dickinson into premature adulthood.

According to Martha Dickinson Bianchi, Emily Dickinson's niece, Edward was

> [a] rather haughty, austere man, shy and gentle, laconic and silent. He dressed in broadcloth at all times, and wore a black beaver hat glossy beyond compare with that of any young beau, and carried a handsome cane to and from his law office on the Main Street of his village. About his neck was wound a black satin stock pinned with a jet and diamond pin.[1]

Although he was "laconic and silent," Edward Dickinson held very strong views and opinions, particularly about the proper roles of men and women. In keeping with the conventions of his time, Edward Dickinson believed that it was a man's job to guard the women around him, a belief he later instilled in his only son Austin.[2] He also believed that women could best serve society as wives and mothers. Though Edward Dickinson supported education for women, like most men of his generation, he felt that the types of books women read should be closely monitored and controlled.

Finding a wife whose sensibility lived up to his expectations was a challenge for Edward Dickinson. However, he pursued marriage with the same fixed determination that he applied to financial and career matters. While attending a chemistry lecture one evening, he sat next to Emily Norcross, who lived in the neighboring town of Monson.[3] Edward Dickinson fixated on the gentle and pretty woman, courting her by letter for two and a half years.[4]

"My Dear [Emily], my heart is with you, and you are constantly in mind," Edward wrote, "I can only give you the parting hand, this morning, & leave the expression of a more ardent attachment till another time –."[5] He expressed his "ardent attachment" over the course of hundreds of letters to Emily Norcross, even though her responses were often discouraging. He also laid out his goals for a future married life:

> May blessings rest upon us, and make us happy – May we be virtuous, intelligent, industrious and by the exercise of every virtue, & the cultivation of every excellence, be esteemed & respected & beloved by all – We must determine to do our duty to each other, & to all our friends, and let others do as they may.[6]

Edward Dickinson's expectations of himself, his wife, and eventually his children were very high. It was not enough for Edward to be "virtuous, intelligent,

[and] industrious" – he also demanded the cultivation of "every" excellence and public acknowledgement "by all." The importance Edward Dickinson placed on "duty to each other" and his need to guide and control his family members show in many of his letters. In a letter written a few years after their marriage, Edward confessed, "I do feel almost guilty to be absent from my little family, during so long a time . . . I know the sacrifice you make in having me absent, is not small – with your natural timidity, & your strong reliance on your husband in time of trouble, I can imagine your suffering."[7]

By calling attention to his wife's "natural timidity" and "strong reliance" upon him, Edward Dickinson reinforces his dominant role in their relationship. During their courtship, Emily Norcross wrote considerably less than Edward. It is possible that she distrusted a passionate pursuit after such a scant acquaintance. After seeing Emily Norcross twice in person, Edward Dickinson proposed marriage.

Emily Norcross seemed hesitant, to say the least, about marrying this dashing and driven man. Some critics suggest that Emily Dickinson's mother projected a facade of compliance but remained independent in thought and action.[8] It is not surprising that her elder daughter would eventually display the same paradoxical mix of compliance and quiet rebellion. In fact, Emily Dickinson may have modeled her self-imposed seclusion on her mother's example; Mrs Dickinson was an invalid for much of her adult life.

Regardless of her reservations, Emily Norcross succumbed to Edward's persistence and pursuit and the couple married on 6 May 1828. Like most women of her time, the newly married Mrs Dickinson left her family, friends, and home to make a new life with her husband. Because Amherst lacked railroad access, she sent her dower by a pair of brindle oxen.

Almost immediately after marriage, the Dickinsons began building their family. Within five years they had three children: William Austin (16 April 1829), Emily Elisabeth (10 December 1830), and Lavinia Norcross (28 February 1833).

The house where the young family lived, and indeed, where Dickinson was born and spent most of her adult life, was known as The Homestead. Built by Dickinson's paternal grandfather, The Homestead was a two-story Federal-style brick home with a property line running straight down the middle. It was not unusual for a home at that time to be owned and occupied by more than one family and "as many as thirteen people" shared The Homestead.[9] Edward Dickinson, his wife Emily, and their children lived in one half of the house. The grandparents, Samuel and Lucretia Dickinson, and Edward's siblings lived in the other half. Both families shared a common kitchen and hearth. Because life in the two-household Homestead was crowded, it was difficult for anyone to have much privacy. The Dickinson children learned to adapt to their close quarters, play without disturbing the other members of the house, and capitalize on any privacy they could find. These were all skills that Dickinson later employed as an adult in order to write poetry.

The Homestead's division into east and west halves not only meant that two families could live there, but also that portions of the house could be sold to different owners. When Edward Dickinson's law practice began to falter, he sold his stake in the house to his cousin, who then sold the entire building.[10] In 1840 the Dickinsons moved to West Street (known today as Pleasant Street), where Emily Dickinson lived from age nine to age twenty-five.[11]

A portrait of the poet as a young girl

When she was nine years old, Dickinson entered Amherst Academy, a school that had recently begun accepting female students. Amherst Academy was founded to provide religious instruction. A typical school day began with prayer, continued with instruction in various academic disciplines, and then concluded with more prayer. While studying at Amherst Academy, Dickinson read a number of religious texts, including Milton's *Paradise Lost*, Edward Young's *Night Thoughts*, and William Cowper's *The Task*.[12] While emphasizing religious instruction, Amherst Academy also offered a rigorous secular education. Dickinson took courses such as English, Latin, geology, algebra, geometry, botany, and history.[13]

Perhaps even more important than facilitating her education, Amherst Academy gave Emily Dickinson opportunities for building friendships. Her first schoolgirl devotions were precursors to the intense literary friendships she would maintain as an adult. In a newsy letter about school, Dickinson wrote, "We really have some most charming young women in school this term. I sha'n't call them anything but women, for women they are in every sense of the word" (*L* 14, no. 6). These statements not only reveal Dickinson's pride in her peers but also a proto-feminist insistence on calling them "women." Among her favorite young women were Abiah Root, Helen Fiske, and Helen Hunt (eventually Helen Hunt Jackson). Her devotion to these friends was steadfast. "I keep your lock of hair as precious as gold," she wrote to Abiah, "I often look at it when I go to my little lot of treasures, and wish the owner of that glossy lock were here" (*L* 9, no. 5).

In addition to her cherished friends, Dickinson also adored her instructors. "You know I am always in love with my teachers," she wrote to Abiah (*L* 45, no. 15). When one of her most beloved teachers married and left teaching, Dickinson tried to sound happy for her teacher, but her 1847 letter reveals conflicting feelings:

> Yet, much as we love her, it seems lonely & strange without "Our dear Miss Adams." I suppose you know she has left Amherst, not again to return as a teacher. It is indeed true, that she is to be married . . . She seemed to be very happy in anticipation of her future prospects, & I hope she will realize all her fond hopes. I cannot bear to think that she will never more wield the sceptre, & sit upon the throne in our venerable schoolhouse, & yet I am glad she is going to have a home of her own & a kind companion to take life's journey with her.   (*L* 45–6, no. 15)

Although Dickinson "cannot bear" to think of her regal teacher leaving, she says what duty demands – she congratulates Miss Adams on achieving a "home of her own" and "a kind companion." However, the language Dickinson uses to discuss Miss Adams shows that a schoolroom can be a woman's kingdom, a place where she can reign, "wield the sceptre," and "sit upon the throne." This is a position of power that Miss Adams will lose when she marries and becomes part of her husband's household. In addition to her sadness over the "dethroning" of a teacher, Dickinson felt "lonely & strange" about being left behind. It was a feeling that would happen again and again throughout her life. Her friendship with Abiah Root, which spanned a decade of long, detail-rich letters, ended in 1854 after Abiah's marriage. Because no known letters between the women exist after that date, it appears that Abiah left her girlhood friend behind when she married, or that Dickinson felt she could not compete with a husband for her friend's affection. As her friends married and moved away, Dickinson felt more abandoned and alone.

School was fun for the young, curious Emily Dickinson. She enjoyed many subjects and acquired information (scientific language, mathematical diction) that would later inform her poetry. She studied botany, and her letters and poems demonstrate an awareness of the scientific names and classifications of many plants and flowers, although she often preferred their common names. Her knowledge of plant names may have come from one of her most treasured school projects – a herbarium, or plant specimen collection. This was a collection of pressed and labeled specimens kept in an 11 by 13 inch leather book. Dickinson carefully pressed and labeled each stem, flower, and leaf, noting the class and order. She collected specimens from forests, fields, and even her own garden. Always a magnanimous and generous friend, she also collected plants, leaves, and wildflowers for her friends' collections.

The herbarium is especially interesting for Dickinson scholars, who see in it the beginning of Dickinson's love of nature, scientific precision, and meticulous observation. The collection of over 400 specimens may also be a precursor to the hand-bound poetry collections, known as fascicles, that Dickinson would assemble as an adult. In fact, as she matured, the boundaries between plants and pages blurred more and more: she wrote poems about flowers, wrapped flowers in poems, and carefully observed and nurtured words and plants alike. One of her favorite flowers was the white saprophytic Indian pipe, an exquisitely delicate and difficult flower to cultivate. There was no way for Dickinson to know that, on 12 November 1890, the very same flowers would grace the title page of the first edition of her published poems.[14]

The garden was a refuge for Emily Dickinson. She doted on her plants, covering them to protect against frost, carefully watering and clipping them, and writing detailed instructions for their care when she was away from home. The garden was an escape from the demands of family, household, and society. It was also a place where Dickinson could observe nature. Many of the living creatures and plants that inhabited her garden – including snakes, bumblebees, and bobolinks – appeared in her poetry. The garden was a place where Dickinson felt she belonged. "I have lately come to the conclusion that I am Eve, alias Mrs. Adam," she joked in a letter to Abiah Root (*L* 24, no. 9). The garden was also a great source of pride for Dickinson. When her brother Austin was in Boston, Dickinson bragged that the splendors of the city could not compare with the splendor of her own garden: "never mind faded forests, Austin, never mind silent fields – *here* is a little forest whose leaf is ever green, here is a *brighter* garden, where not a frost has been, in its unfading flowers I hear the bright bee hum, prithee, my Brother, into *my* garden come!" (*L* 149, no. 58).

Although as an adult Emily Dickinson restricted her life to her home in Amherst, as a young woman she traveled several times to large cities in the area. In 1846, when she was only fifteen years old, Dickinson traveled alone to Boston. She sent a letter to Abiah Root describing her Boston adventures:

> Father & Mother thought a journey would be of service to me &
> accordingly, I left for Boston week before last. I had a delightful ride in
> the cars & am now quietly settled down, if there can be such a state in
> the city. I am visiting my aunt's family & am happy . . . I have been to
> Mount Auburn, to the Chinese Museum, to Bunker hill. I have attended
> 2 concerts, & 1 Horticultural exhibition. I have been upon the top of the
> State house & almost everywhere that you can imagine. Have you ever
> been to Mount Auburn? If not you can form but slight conception – of
> the "City of the dead."   (*L* 36, no. 13)

Modern readers tend to think that Dickinson was always a shy, self-sequestered recluse, but in fact she traveled with her father, lived with relatives for extended periods of time, and had many friends. Her description of the city is particularly interesting, given her ongoing interest in death and the afterlife. Boston was a "City of the dead" to Dickinson in multiple senses: it was a site of American history and Dickinson arrived the week of a heat wave in the city that contributed to the deaths of over 100 people (*L* 38, no. 13).

After completing her program at Amherst Academy, Dickinson entered Mount Holyoke Female Seminary in South Hadley in 1847. Founded by Mary Lyon, the Seminary sought to instill religious values and prepare young women to become suitable wives and mothers.[15] The sixteen-year-old Dickinson felt homesick in this strictly controlled environment.[16] "It has been nearly six weeks since I left home & that is a longer time, than I was ever away from home before now. I was very homesick for a few days & it seemed to me I could not live here," she wrote on 6 November 1847 (*L* 53, no. 18). In many ways, Dickinson's Mount Holyoke letters could just as easily be e-mails sent home by a typical college freshman today. She complains about dorm food, savors care packages from home, keeps secrets from her parents, and tries to sound independent even though she is homesick. After a visit from her brother Austin, Dickinson wrote,

> I watched you until you were out of sight Saturday evening & then went to my room & looked over my treasures & surely no miser ever counted his heaps of gold, with more satisfaction than I gazed upon the presents from home.
> The cake, gingerbread, pie, & peaches are all devoured, but the – apples – chestnuts & grapes still remain & will I hope for some time.
>
> (*L* 47–8, no. 16)

The artificial cloister of Dickinson's education must have been frustrating. She longed to know details about the world outside Mount Holyoke and wrote letters to Austin that simultaneously begged for news and poked fun at her own isolation:

> Wont you please to tell me when you answer my letter who the candidate for President is? I have been trying to find out ever since I came here & have not yet succeeded. I dont know anything more about affairs in the world, than if I was in a trance . . . Has the Mexican war terminated yet & how? Are we beat? Do you know of any nation about to besiege South Hadley? If so, do inform me of it, for I would be glad of a chance to escape, if we are to be stormed. I suppose Miss Lyon. would furnish us all with daggers & order us to fight for our lives, in case such perils should befall us.   (*L* 49, no. 16)

Like many of her letters, this one demonstrates Dickinson's sharp wit and ability to discuss serious issues (longing for knowledge about politics and war) alongside playful banter (a hypothetical nation storming her inconsequential school town).

Dickinson's roommate at Mount Holyoke was her cousin, Emily Lavinia Norcross.[17] Like many of Dickinson's friends and relatives, Emily Lavinia Norcross suffered from "consumption," or tuberculosis.[18] The disease was not well understood at the time, and people did not know that it was transmittable by air. Because of Dickinson's proximity to her cousin and her own faltering health, some critics have surmised that Dickinson was also infected with TB. In May of her first year at Mount Holyoke, Dickinson became sick and developed a cough. Her 16 May 1848 letter describes her effort to conceal her illness from her parents as well as how the secret was disclosed:

> I had not been very well all winter, but had not written home about it, lest the folks should take me home. During the week following examinations, a friend from Amherst came over and spent a week with me, and when that friend returned home, father and mother were duly notified of the state of my health. Have you so treacherous a friend?
>
> Now knowing that I was to be reported at home, you can imagine my amazement and consternation when Saturday of the same week Austin arrived in full sail, with orders from head-quarters to bring me home at all events. At first I had recourse to words, and a desperate battle with those weapons was waged for a few moments, between my *Sophomore* brother and myself. Finding words of no avail, I next resorted to tears . . . As you can imagine, Austin was victorious, and poor, defeated I was led off in triumph.   (*L* 65, no. 23)

In this letter, Dickinson's frustration at the revelation of her illness by a well-intentioned but "treacherous" friend and subsequent kidnapping by her brother is evident. The letter also exhibits rarely voiced but persistent bitterness toward her more powerful, privileged, and "victorious" brother. She patronizes Austin by mocking his seniority. Even though he has completed more years in college than she has, he is still only a second-year student. She may also be playing with the etymology of sophomore, which is a combination of the Greek words for "wise" as well as "foolish."

While Dickinson was studying at Mount Holyoke, Austin was preparing for a career in law. All three Dickinson children wrote poetry and, like his sisters, Austin was "a hero-worshipper, a partisan, and a lover of all the rare and noble books."[19] However, while Austin was encouraged to read books, his sisters' reading was carefully monitored: "[Father] buys me many Books – but begs me not to read them – because he fears they joggle the Mind," Dickinson wrote (*L* 404, no. 261).

However, Austin would hide the forbidden books so Dickinson could read them. For example, he tucked a copy of Henry Wadsworth Longfellow's

Kavanagh under a piano cover.[20] Although she gleefully conspired with her brother, Dickinson's early letters reveal that she also felt threatened by Austin's encroachment upon her poetic territory. In a letter to her brother, she sarcastically announced, "And Austin is a Poet, Austin writes a psalm. Out of the way, Pegasus, Olympus enough 'to him,' and just say to those 'nine muses' that we have done with them!" (*L* 235, no. 110). As a middle child in a tight-knit family, writing was one of the few ways Dickinson was able to distinguish herself from her older "Brother Pegasus" and younger sister Vinnie.

Early ambitions, difficult changes

Although Dickinson established herself as "the writer" in the family, her future remained uncertain. It was acceptable for a woman in the early nineteenth century to work as a teacher, nurse, or governess, but none of these occupations appealed to Dickinson.[21] Even if she had had the audacity to defy her father and become a "literary woman," there were few opportunities for a woman interested in writing and literature whose poetic style was as elliptical and complex as hers.

Dickinson's literary guides were the authors she read at night in her room. She hung pictures of Thomas Carlyle, Elizabeth Barrett Browning, and George Eliot in her bedroom.[22] In 1849, a friend lent Dickinson a copy of *Jane Eyre*, a controversial new book published by a mysterious author named Currer Bell. The author's name was a pseudonym and many book reviewers and critics hypothesized about the author's true name and gender. Critics complained that *Jane Eyre*'s heroine was too self-reliant, independent, and common to be a moral model for women. Dickinson was aware of this controversy, but she loved the novel. When she returned the borrowed book, she enclosed a bouquet of leaves and the following note:

> Mr. Bowdoin.
>   If all these leaves were altars, and on every one a prayer that Currer Bell might be saved – and you were God – would you answer it?
>
> (*L* 77, no. 28)

In her typical style, Dickinson does not simply thank her friend for lending the book, but instead sends a witty and allusive epigram about the book itself. The note could mean that Dickinson wants Currer Bell to be "saved" and live a long life in order to write more books as pleasing as *Jane Eyre*. The letter could also be Dickinson's nod toward the controversial nature of the book and her own belief that Bell had not offended God and deserved to be "saved." She goes so far as to put her friend Bowdoin in the position of God to pass judgment on Currer Bell. She also puns on the word "leaves," playing with both the pages of the book and the leaves from the bouquet.

The controversy over *Jane Eyre* reached new heights in 1851, when newspapers revealed that Currer Bell was actually a woman – Charlotte Brontë. Dickinson's devotion to this controversial novel and its female author was intense. When her father gave her a pet dog, an enormous Newfoundland, Dickinson named him Carlo, after a character's dog in *Jane Eyre*.[23]

As Dickinson's own interest in writing increased, her fascination with prominent, controversial women writers also grew. In August of 1859, the *Republican* unmasked the author of *Adam Bede*, another novel that Dickinson greatly admired. The public learned that George Eliot was actually an English woman named Marian Evans. The revelations of Currer Bell and George Eliot occurred at impressionable times for Dickinson, then in her twenties.

Although her health improved, Emily Dickinson's college career was over. "Father has decided not to send me to Holyoke another year, so this is my *last* term," she wrote to Abiah Root (*L* 66, no. 23). She returned to her family's second home on West Street, adjacent to the village cemetery. "Yesterday as I sat by the north window the funeral train entered the open gate of the church yard," Dickinson wrote (*L* 31, no. 11). The vantage point of the West Street bedroom provided ample material for later poems: she observed funeral processions from her window, took note of individual mourners and families, and contemplated the nature of death and the afterlife.

Although the West Street home was comfortable, Edward Dickinson was determined to restore the prestige of the family and he soon bought back The Homestead, remodeled it, and built a home – The Evergreens – for his son Austin on the same lot. Once the family returned to The Homestead in 1855, however, new problems emerged. Dickinson's mother became an invalid, shifting the primary household responsibilities to her daughters. From an early age, Dickinson learned that pain and loss were an inextricable part of life and that "it was women and not men who were expected to deal with sickness and death."[24] The twenty-four-year-old Dickinson and her mother reversed roles, with the young woman taking responsibility for housekeeping and caretaking. In fact, the Dickinson daughters would take care of their ailing mother for the next twenty-seven years.

Running the household and entertaining guests were particularly demanding tasks for the sisters. Because Edward Dickinson was an attorney and served on the Massachusetts Legislature, the house often hosted clients, lawyers, speakers, students, politicians, and clergymen. Dickinson described their home's popularity as "the usual rush of callers, and this beleaguered family as yet in want of time" (*L* 275, no. 145). The Dickinson women were frequently alone as well, due to Edward's speaking engagements and travel. Although he was often away from home while serving in the Massachusetts Legislature, Edward Dickinson tried to control his home life with the same strict order he applied to his public life. Despite his wife's wishes, he arranged for a male lodger to look after the family and sent many prescriptive letters. "I trust you will be prudent, and not expose yourself to cold, or the *evening air*," Edward wrote to his wife.[25] He was also adamant about his daughters remaining indoors: "they must be very careful about taking cold, in this pleasant weather – Lavinia, particularly, is exposed to croup, & must be closely watched . . . *You must not go into the yard, yourself,* on any account – there is no necessity for it, and you *must not do it.*"[26] In fact, many of the activities that Emily Dickinson enjoyed, including taking walks, picking wildflowers, and going to school, were prohibited by her father's letters. "Do not overdo – nor exert yourself too much – don't go out, evenings, on any account – nor too much, in the afternoon," Edward wrote his wife. "It is better for you, in cold weather, to stay at home, pretty much . . . Don't let Austin be out too much in cold, stormy weather. Emily must not go to school, at all."[27]

Edward Dickinson's stern edicts had a powerful impact. According to Martha Dickinson Bianchi, the patriarch "evidenced his displeasure by taking his hat and cane and passing out the door in silence, leaving an emptiness indicative of reproof, a wordless censure more devastating to her [Emily] than any judgment day."[28] In 1851, when Dickinson was twenty, she wrote to her friend Abiah Root about neglecting a curfew and her father's frightening response: "after tea I went to see Sue – had a nice little visit with her – then went to see Emily Fowler, and arrived home at 9 – found Father is great agitation at my protracted stay – and mother and Vinnie in tears, for fear that he would kill me" (*L* 111, no. 42). The hyperbole Dickinson uses in this letter to describe her father's wrath ("would kill me") sounds surprisingly familiar to modern ears. Dickinson was a young adult, barely out of her teens, challenging her father by staying out late with friends.

Emily Dickinson's relationship with her father was one of the most influential of her life. Nearly 100 years later, the American poet Sylvia Plath became famous for the ways in which her paternal relationship influenced her poetry. Although Emily Dickinson's relationship with her father was not venomous, as Plath's was, both poets experienced conflicting emotions for their distant, driven fathers. After Edward Dickinson's death, Dickinson wrote, "His Heart was pure and terrible and I think no other like it exists" (*L* 528, no. 418). As a young woman, Dickinson feared her over-protective, domineering father, but as she matured, she was able to negotiate with him, taking the largest bedroom in the house for her own and retreating from everyday society. It seems that Edward Dickinson and his talented elder daughter came to a tacit agreement about her unusual talents.

The family's financial status was crucial to Emily Dickinson's growth as a poet. The essential duties required to maintain a household in the early to mid-nineteenth century included purchasing goods, growing vegetables, baking, cooking, cleaning, laundering, ironing, sewing, mending, maintaining heat and light, providing pumped water, and nursing the sick – all chores that had to be divided between Emily and her sister Lavinia. Expectations of their brother, however, were different. Because he was male, Austin was assumed to be stronger, healthier, and more fit than his sisters. He also received preferential treatment because he was the eldest and the only one able to pass on the Dickinson name.[29] Austin was obligated to follow in his father's footsteps and have a law career. His sisters, although given a year's experience of higher education, were expected to maintain the household and eventually marry. Instead, both girls dedicated their lives to the household and each other.

Emily Dickinson could not have developed her art without a release from many of the domestic duties expected of a nineteenth-century American woman. Her sister Lavinia helped provide that release. Lavinia took on extra chores to give Emily time to write and helped keep the peace between her family members. When Emily wanted to remain in her room in privacy, Lavinia graciously and diplomatically turned visitors away. Lavinia also carried calling cards and messages from the outside world to her sister's bedroom, keeping Emily up to date on news and gossip. Like her brother and sister, Lavinia also wrote poetry but she devoted most of her efforts to furthering Emily's talents. Martha Dickinson Bianchi fondly remembers her Aunt Vinnie as a powerful domestic presence: she "knew where everything was, from a lost quotation to a last year's muffler. It was she who remembered to have the fruit picked for canning, or the seeds kept for next year's planting, or the perfunctory letters written to the aunts."[30] When hordes of visitors and speakers descended upon The Homestead and The Evergreens, Lavinia played hostess, organizing the food and facilitating conversation. Between her mother's illness and her sister's disinclination toward company, Lavinia took on the responsibility of running the household, often at the expense of her own desires. She sacrificed many of her own wishes and dreams for the benefit of her family, particularly for her older sister. As Martha Dickinson Bianchi suggests, "If Emily had been less Emily, Lavinia might have been more Lavinia."[31]

Preceptors

In 1848, when Emily Dickinson was seventeen, she found the first of her many male mentors: Benjamin Franklin Newton, a young attorney who studied under Edward Dickinson. Newton was nine years older than Dickinson and had fresh and invigorating ideas that stood in stark contrast to the more traditional religious and literary views of most people in Amherst. Newton and Dickinson became friends, engaging in long conversations about literature and aesthetics. He also gave Dickinson her first copy of Ralph Waldo Emerson's 1847 *Poems*.[32] Unfortunately, the Dickinson–Newton letters have not survived. However, Dickinson wrote a letter after Newton's death that describes his influence upon her: "Mr Newton became to me a gentle, yet grave Preceptor, teaching me what to read, what authors to admire, what was most grand or beautiful in nature, and that sublimer lesson, a faith in things unseen" (*L* 282, no. 153). Dickinson's use of the term "Preceptor" has biographical resonance – it is the same term she used to describe the highly educated, refined, and artistically sensitive men whom she chose as her tutors, teachers, mentors, and literary guides throughout her life.

Dickinson befriended another important male "Preceptor" while traveling with her father in Philadelphia. She visited the Arch Street Presbyterian church and heard the Reverend Charles Wadsworth speak. Wadsworth had a deep bass voice and delivered striking, persuasive lectures. He made such an impression upon Dickinson that she wrote to him seeking guidance. He responded and their friendship began.

In 1856, yet another important man joined the ranks of Dickinson's Preceptors. Samuel Bowles was the owner and editor of the *Springfield Republican* and close friend of Austin and his wife Susan. While visiting and corresponding with the couple, Bowles began to notice the shy woman in the house next door. Over time, his friendship with Dickinson developed through long, personal letters.

Perhaps the greatest of Emily Dickinson's male Preceptors was Thomas Wentworth Higginson. A former Unitarian minister with a degree in divinity from Harvard, Higginson was a writer and fervent supporter of women's rights and Abolition.[33] Like Samuel Bowles, Higginson was also a literary editor. In 1862 Higginson edited the *Atlantic Monthly*, a magazine which the Dickinsons received and read. In April, he published an article, "Letter to a Young Contributor," which offered advice for beginning writers. Dickinson read the article and was so moved by it that she immediately wrote a letter to Higginson asking, "Are you too deeply occupied to say if my Verse is alive?" (*L* 403, no. 260). She bravely included four of her own poems, "Safe in their Alabaster Chambers," "The nearest Dream recedes unrealized," "We play at Paste," and "I'll tell you how the Sun rose," and asked Higginson for his impression of them. Higginson replied and the famous friendship began. By her third letter to the editor, Dickinson asked, "But, will you be my Preceptor, Mr. Higginson?" (*L* 409, no. 265). Higginson acted as a guide and friend for Dickinson, continuing a correspondence that lasted until the month of her death.

Newton, Wadsworth, Bowles, and Higginson provided Dickinson with literary guidance and support. They also acted as father figures, friends, and possibly romantic interests. She sought their approval, but when her instincts told her that their advice would lead her astray, as it did when Higginson criticized her poetry, she often chose to have confidence in her own ideas.

Many critics have theorized that one of Dickinson's male Preceptors was "Master," a lover who appears in a series of romantic letters. The Master letters are a collection of three composed (but not necessarily mailed) letters that were found among Dickinson's papers after her death. The first was probably written in 1858, the second in 1861, and the last in 1862. In these letters, a woman who refers to herself as Daisy expresses deep longing for someone she calls Master. The intended recipient may have been one of Dickinson's male friends, an imaginary projection of Dickinson's self, or even the woman who was the most important friend in Dickinson's life – Susan Huntington Gilbert.

"Sister Sue"

Emily Dickinson and Susan Huntington Gilbert met when they were both teenagers. Susan shared Dickinson's love of literature, gardening, recipes, and nature, as well as her dislike of chores and household duties. Dickinson greatly trusted Susan, valuing her opinions and advice, and the two participated in an intense friendship that spanned five decades. Dickinson was eager for a personal connection to replace the friends who had married and moved away, and Susan, orphaned at a young age, was just as eager to become a part of a family. Of all the friends and relatives that Dickinson wrote to during her life, she wrote the most letters to her "Sister" Sue.

Eventually Austin fell in love with Susan and they were engaged in 1853. The young couple married in 1856 and moved into The Evergreens. Susan Dickinson was delighted to live so close to her friend. Interestingly, even though she lived next door, Dickinson still sent Susan letters.

Dickinson's close connection to Susan is evident from the poet's 1858 poem:

One Sister have I in our house,
And one, a hedge away.
There's only one recorded,
But both belong to me.

One came the road that I came –
And wore my last year's gown –
The other, as a bird her nest,
Builded our hearts among.

She did not sing as we did –
It was a different tune –
Herself to her a music
As Bumble bee of June.

Today is far from Childhood –
But up and down the hills
I held her hand the tighter –
Which shortened all the miles –

And still her hum
The years among,
Deceives the Butterfly;
Still in her Eye
The Violets lie
Mouldered this many May.

I spilt the dew –
But took the morn –
I chose this single star –
From out the wide night's numbers –
Sue – forevermore!

(*P* 12–13, no. 14)

In this poem, Dickinson acknowledges that, according to biological standards, she has one sister, Lavinia – the "only one" recorded in history. However, the poem shows that the actions one takes, not the genes in one's blood, define true sisterhood. Sue's compassion, friendship, and love transcend mere biology, making her "belong" to Dickinson as a sister.

Lavinia is a "real" sister in the sense that she came from the same parents ("came the road that I came"), wears hand-me-downs from her older sibling ("wore my last year's gown"), and shares personality characteristics with Dickinson ("sing as we did"). However, despite Sue's differences ("It was a different tune"), she became firmly attached to the poet's heart ("as a bird her nest, /

Builded our hearts among"). What is perhaps most remarkable about this poem is that Dickinson *chooses* her own family. Among a galaxy of possibilities, she "chose this single star" and made Sue her own "forevermore."

The comparison of Susan Dickinson with a star in the sky is romantic: Dickinson seems to be playing Astrophel to Sue's Stella. The woman who lived "a hedge away" with Austin was intricately connected to Emily Dickinson, so much so that some scholars have argued that the two women had an erotic relationship. Regardless of the definition of their love, the affection was clearly mutual. As Susan's daughter, Martha Dickinson Bianchi, writes, Susan "recognized her genius from the first, and hoarded every scrap Emily sent her."[34]

Dickinson showered love and attention on her new sister-in-law and had even greater cause for celebration in 1861, when Austin and Susan had their first child, named after his grandfather, Edward Dickinson. The poet's delight in becoming an aunt is evident in the whimsical note she sent to Susan shortly after the birth:

> Is it true, dear Sue?
> Are there *two?*
> I should'nt like to come
> For fear of joggling Him!
> If I could shut him up
> In a Coffee Cup,
> Or tie him to a pin
> Till I got in –
> Or make him fast
> To "Toby's" fist –
> Hist! Whist! I'd come.
>   (*L* 373, no. 232)

In this letter-poem, Dickinson reacts to the baby's birth as if Susan herself were twinned: there are now "two" of her "dear Sue." Dickinson's delight in the baby's birth is checked by an overwhelming fear of harming him; like many new aunts who have never had children of their own, she worries about "joggling" the newborn by holding him. The poem also emphasizes the fragility of the newborn by exaggerating his size; the baby in the poem is small enough to fit inside a cup, weak enough to be held by a pin, and tender enough to be held by a cat's paw (Toby's fist). Although the note congratulates Sue on giving birth and celebrates the new baby, it is also an apology – the poem provides fanciful rationalizations for why Dickinson does not leave her home and visit the new baby next door.

Dickinson positively doted upon each of Austin and Susan's children as her own: Edward (Ned) in 1861, Martha (Mattie) in 1866, and Thomas Gilbert (Gib) in 1875. In many ways, Dickinson stayed within her brother's and sister-in-law's orbit: she loved their children as her own and befriended many of their friends. As Martha Dickinson Bianchi notes, Dickinson's girlhood friends, Abiah Wood, Eliza Coleman, Abiah Root, Martha Gilbert, Emily Fowler, and Helen Fiske all married and left Amherst to start new lives with their husbands.[35] In her letters to girlhood friends, Dickinson half-jokingly accused them of abandoning her. Many of the new friends of her adult life came through her father, Austin, and Sue.

A "Woman – white – to be"

The establishment of literary Preceptors, the luxury of domestic help, the support of a beloved father and sister, the return to the family home, and the arrival of Susan Dickinson all served as resources for Dickinson's poetry. Perhaps these events laid the groundwork for the creative bursts to follow. According to Dickinson's first major biographer, Ralph W. Franklin, in the summer of 1858 Dickinson began an immense project similar to her childhood herbarium. She began collecting all of her poems, copying them in ink on folded stationery, stitching the pages together by hand, and destroying the original drafts. Although the fascicles were meticulously collected, Dickinson's organizational method is unknown. Because the poems were unthreaded and reordered several times after her death, Dickinson's original order is an area of speculation. However, the best modern re-creations indicate that the poems were not necessarily in chronological or thematic order. She made forty fascicles and ten more unthreaded sets that together held about 800 poems.[36] Editor Thomas H. Johnson called the period from 1861 to 1865 the "flood" years of Dickinson's poetic production. For example, in 1862, her most productive year, Dickinson averaged a poem a day.[37] Significantly, these "flood" years coincide with the years of the American Civil War.

The next phase of Dickinson's life is the most famous and perhaps most analyzed and debated aspect of her biography. Although always separated from society by her intellect and unusual disposition, Dickinson became more and more removed from the social norms of her community. From the 1860s onward, she began to dress all in white, especially after Edward Dickinson's death in 1874. Whether the choice of dress was practical (white was easy to launder and mend), symbolic (mourning, virginity), or a type of self-chosen uniform (poet, bride), the clothing was different and therefore noticed and mythologized through small-town gossip. Sometime around 1869, when she was thirty-eight years old, Dickinson chose to remain permanently on the grounds of The Homestead and The Evergreens, never leaving the property and receding from public life completely. "I do not cross my Father's ground to any House or town," she explained to Thomas Wentworth Higginson (*L* 460, no. 330).

What caused Dickinson to seclude herself from society? This is the question that continues to perplex each new generation of Dickinson scholars. In the 1800s, pregnant women were expected to separate themselves from society, a custom which the Victorians called "confinement." One could argue that Dickinson took up this ritual and transformed it from something negative to something positive – confining herself in order to give birth to her poetry. Readers, fans, historians, and critics of Dickinson will never know for certain the motivations behind Dickinson's self-induced seclusion and creative outburst. Although her actions may have seemed radical for her time, they were also necessary for her art. She liberated herself from time-consuming social events such as lectures, parties, picnics, fairs, receptions, church socials, weddings, baptisms, and funerals. It is also important to note that, though Dickinson remained physically separate from society, she was still very much emotionally and intellectually invested in her family, her correspondence, and news of the world.

In fact, shortly after this time, Dickinson may have received a marriage proposal from a close friend she had known for many years. The man that many biographers have called the love of Dickinson's life was Otis Phillips Lord, a friend of Edward Dickinson. He was a judge on the Massachusetts Supreme Judicial Court and was closer to Dickinson's father's age than Dickinson's. However, the two began a friendship of their own, fed over time by increasingly affectionate letters. What began as a friendship became a "late-life romance," but the exact dates are unknown because most of the correspondence between the two was destroyed.[38] Although Judge Lord and Dickinson were close, her father's disapproval and her own reservations about marriage and leaving her family would have prevented any marriage.

For Dickinson, The Homestead and its grounds had always functioned as a source of imagination, companionship, and a shelter from the demands of the outside world. One could argue that as she grew as a poet, she spent more and more time in her room because it was the space in which she created poetry. It also allowed her to see only the people who were most important to her and exclude the time-consuming yet meaningless pleasantries that are expected in everyday society. Her decision to remove herself from society is reflected in the following poem, written in 1862:

> The Soul selects her own Society –
> Then – shuts the Door –
> To her divine Majority –
> Present no more –
>
> Unmoved – she notes the Chariots – pausing –
> At her low Gate –
> Unmoved – an Emperor be kneeling
> Upon her Mat –
>
> I've known her – from an ample nation –
> Choose one –
> Then – close the Valves of her attention –
> Like Stone –   (*P* 143, no. 303)

The number of people Dickinson allowed through "the Valves of her attention" grew smaller each year. Whether a visitor be a friend or "Emperor," each was treated the same; Dickinson allowed very few people into her immediate surroundings, but Thomas Wentworth Higginson was one of the chosen few. The description of their first momentous meeting is preserved in a letter Higginson wrote to his wife:

> A step like a pattering child's in entry & in glided a little plain woman with two smooth bands of reddish hair . . . in a very plain & exquisitely white pique & a blue worsted shawl. She came to me with two day lilies which she put in a sort of childlike way into my hand & said "These are my introduction" in a soft frightened breathless childlike voice – & added under her breath Forgive me if I am frightened; I never see strangers & hardly know what I say – but she talked soon & thenceforward continuously.   (*L* 473, no. 342a)

The initial hesitancy and childlike shyness, pure white attire, and presentation of flowers in lieu of words were all hallmark characteristics of Emily Dickinson. It is humorous, however, to notice that once the "breathless child" became comfortable with the physical presence of the Preceptor she had long admired through letters, her loquacity exhausted him. "I never was with any one who drained my nerve power so much," Higginson noted. "Without touching her, she drew from me. I am glad not to live near her" (*L* 476, no. 342b). His surprisingly humorous descriptions of Dickinson reveal the difficulty Lavinia and Sue must have had living in close proximity to such a sensitive creative force. Recalling that first meeting for the October 1891 issue of the *Atlantic Monthly*, Higginson wrote, "She was much too enigmatical a being for me to solve in an hour's interview, and an instinct told me that the slightest attempt at direct cross-examination would make her withdraw into her shell; I could only sit still and watch."[39] Emily Dickinson met with Higginson again on 3 December 1873. During this visit, she handed him a *Daphne odora*, a sweet-smelling winter flower. She also gave him a copy of a poem, "The Wind begun to rock and Grass," which has since been lost.

Although her interior, intellectual, and poetic lives were blossoming, Dickinson's physical health was rapidly declining. Everyone in the Dickinson family suffered from some type of eye problem, but her eye problems were the most serious. Early in 1861, Dickinson's vision changed drastically and she traveled to Boston for treatment in 1864 and 1865. Because she relied upon her eyesight for reading and writing, the pain and loss of vision must have been particularly threatening to her.

In addition to her physical troubles, Dickinson endured increasing hardships in her personal life. In 1874, while giving a speech, Edward Dickinson collapsed and died soon after. His family did not even have the chance to say goodbye. As she wrote to Higginson, the morning her father left for his trip, the forty-three-year-old Dickinson "woke him for the train – and saw him no more" (*L* 528, no. 418).

Although the death of Edward Dickinson was a great blow to the family, the birth of Austin and Susan's third child, Thomas Gilbert, may have eased some of their heartache. Dickinson was greatly fond of all the children, but was particularly attached to Gib. Although their Aunt Emily remained firmly secluded in her bedroom and turned away visitors, the young children were able to pester her for sweets and treats, which she loaded into a basket on a rope and lowered from her window.

Over the next decade, Dickinson suffered the loss of many close friends: Samuel Bowles died in 1878 followed by Reverend Wadsworth in 1879 and her mother, Emily Norcross Dickinson, in 1882. At fifty-one, Dickinson had lost both parents. In the following years, she mourned the loss of her beloved Judge Lord as well as her friend and admirer Helen Hunt Jackson. However, the most difficult death to overcome was the death of her nephew Gib, who died of typhoid fever on 5 October 1883. He was only eight years old when he died and Dickinson was so stricken with grief that some biographers claim that Gib's death was the beginning of Dickinson's own decline.[40]

As the Dickinsons struggled with the loss of so many friends and relatives, strain among the surviving family members increased. The most serious conflict arose from a romantic liaison between Austin Dickinson and a much younger, married woman, Mabel Loomis Todd, who had moved with her husband to Amherst in 1881. The size of the community and the proximity of The Evergreens to The Homestead meant that this affair could not remain a secret for long. Dickinson and her sister Lavinia probably knew of this liaison, as Austin sometimes met Mabel Loomis Todd in The Homestead while his wife Sue was in The Evergreens. If the Dickinson sisters were critical of the trysts between Austin and his mistress within The Homestead walls, their disapproval was not voiced, perhaps because of their financial dependence on their brother. Loyalty to family members was also a primary concern for the Dickinsons.

With the death of their father in 1874, followed by the death of their mother eight years later, Austin was left as owner of both The Homestead and The Evergreens. Regardless of whether or not Dickinson condoned her brother's behavior, Susan Dickinson read Dickinson's silence as approval. The pain and scandal caused by the affair between Austin and Mabel Loomis Todd would eventually play a role in the controversial first publication of Dickinson's letters and poems – Sue refused to share her copies of poems and letters with Mabel, and Mabel edited references to Sue out of the published letters.

In the last years of her life, Dickinson spoke to friends, visitors, and even a doctor from behind the safety of a door or curtain. She even remained in her upstairs bedroom during her father's funeral in the house, listening to the service below. Like many who admired Dickinson and became part of her inner circle, Mabel "came to know her principally through the sound of her voice."[41] Although Mabel became the first published editor and authority of Dickinson's poetry, she never saw Dickinson in person.

The stress of the family conflict, the deaths of her parents and many of her friends (thirty-one had died of tuberculosis alone), and failing health took their toll on Dickinson.[42] On 14 June 1884 she collapsed in The Homestead kitchen. She continued to have fainting spells, and on 13 May 1886 Dickinson permanently lost consciousness. Her family members gathered around Dickinson and were with her when she died at The Homestead on 15 May 1886. Her official cause of death was "Bright's Disease," an umbrella term for a variety of kidney disorders. Some modern critics, however, have hypothesized that her symptoms indicated hypertension or high blood pressure, leading to syncope (fainting) and eventually stroke.[43]

Susan Dickinson arranged for her sister-in-law's burial. A local Amherst mortician, Ellery Strickland, prepared Emily Dickinson's body.[44] A self-described "Woman – white – to be," Dickinson was placed in a white casket wearing a white flannel robe, clothed in death by the same color she wore in life. Violets and cypripedium were placed across her throat and heliotropes were tucked into her hand. Dickinson left specific directions for her funeral procession, which her family honored. She chose six Irish workers from The Homestead to act as pallbearers and asked to be carried through the back door and into the garden, through a meadow, and into the cemetery. In doing so, Dickinson avoided a public funeral procession and retained in death the privacy that she so carefully protected in life.[45]

Only close friends and relatives were able to pay their respects to Dickinson. Thomas Wentworth Higginson, who had so few opportunities to view his beloved friend while she was alive, was moved by her beauty in death. At fifty-five years old, Dickinson still had a head full of auburn hair and smooth, youthful skin. The funeral, like Dickinson's own life, was modest and private. It was held in The Homestead library on 19 May 1886. In honor of his beloved, elusive friend, Higginson read one of Dickinson's favorite poems by Emily Brontë, "No Coward Soul is Mine." This poem, written on 2 January 1846, was Brontë's last. When Higginson stood in The Homestead library and read the final line, "And what thou art may never be destroyed," he was comforting Dickinson's survivors, but perhaps he was also indicating his faith in Dickinson's poetic legacy.[46]

The initials "EED" were carved upon Dickinson's headstone. However, in the early twentieth century, Sue's daughter, Martha Dickinson Bianchi, chose a new tombstone.[47] The new epitaph read simply, "Called Back." The phrase referred to Dickinson's last known letter, which she wrote to her cousins Louise and Frances Norcross. Written just a few weeks before her death, the letter read, "Little Cousins, Called back. Emily" (L 906, no. 1046). Dickinson had read Hugh Conway's popular novella Called Back and was playfully punning. She may have been joking with her cousins that she could not write a longer letter because members of the household were calling for her. On a more serious note, she may have realized that her illness was becoming more severe and that death was calling. Because Dickinson described Called Back as "a haunting story . . . 'greatly Impressive to me,'" it seems appropriate that the phrase should appear in her last known letter and, subsequently, on her gravestone (L 855–6, no. 962).

After Emily Dickinson's death, Lavinia went through her sister's possessions and found pages and pages of writing – far more than anyone knew existed. Several months after her death, the poems and letters that were Emily Dickinson's life's work began a new life of their own.

Chapter 2

Context

Religious culture: Puritanism, the Great Awakenings,
   and revivals *24*
Industrialization and the individual *27*
Political culture: expansion and the antebellum period *28*
Social movements: Abolition and women's rights *30*
Philosophical reactions: Transcendentalism *32*
The Civil War *34*

Emily Dickinson was writing at an explosive time in American history. A brief snapshot of the events of her lifetime includes the Mexican–American War, the California Gold Rush, the first women's rights convention, Harriet Tubman's escape on the Underground Railroad, the publication of *Uncle Tom's Cabin*, the Civil War, and the shootings of two Presidents. By the time Dickinson was born, the country had steam-powered locomotives and gas lamps, which were soon followed by the revolver, telegraph, bicycles, anesthesia, and dynamite. In addition to political and technological advances, a religious and spiritual revolution was also gaining momentum. Emily Dickinson was not writing in a vacuum: she was both a product of her culture and an active participant through discussions, letters, and poetry. In fact, three of her poems appeared in *Drum Beat*, a Brooklyn newspaper that raised funds for the Union effort. Contrary to the myth of the secluded poet who locked herself away from the rest of the world, Dickinson was aware of local and national events and used political and cultural tropes in her poetry. As the country struggled to define itself and the rights of its citizens, she struggled to establish her identity as a woman and writer. Emily Dickinson acted out historical and cultural movements in a personal way.

Religious culture: Puritanism, the Great Awakenings, and revivals

After learning that her brother Austin had enjoyed a somewhat scandalous meeting with Susan Huntington Gilbert in a Boston hotel, Emily Dickinson jokingly wrote, "Am glad our Pilgrim Fathers got safely out of the way, before such shocking times!" (*L* 235, no. 110). In this letter, Dickinson not only teases her brother, but also reveals a truth about her religious environment. Although they were "safely out of the way," the Pilgrims' influence was still very much felt in Amherst during the "shocking times" of Dickinson's life.

In fact, much of the religious context of Emily Dickinson's nineteenth-century Amherst was tied to its Puritan heritage. The Puritans were English citizens who believed in the need to "purify" the Church of England, which they felt too closely resembled the Catholic Church. Religious tensions in England pushed the Puritans to leave England and help establish colonies in the New World.

The Puritans founded the Massachusetts Bay Colony in 1630. Nathaniel Dickinson, an ancestor of Emily Dickinson, was one of the first Puritans to settle in Amherst.[1] The Puritans hoped to reform the Church by destroying organizational hierarchies and eliminating ornamental rituals such as the Catholic Mass. They eventually broke completely from the Church of England and founded the Congregational Church. Congregationalists believed that individual church power structures should depend on the local congregation, not on the English king or archbishop.

Adherents to the Congregational Church followed the Reformation ideal of salvation through faith rather than works. They believed in original sin (resulting from the fall from grace in the Garden of Eden), a vengeful God, and a heaven reserved for only those chosen by God. They followed the ideas of Calvinism, a set of doctrinal beliefs modeled on John Calvin, a sixteenth-century reformer. According to Calvinism, God chose which people would be saved by faith. The chosen entered into a covenant with God and enacted it in their daily lives. In order to proclaim their status as chosen, Congregationalists of the eighteenth century publicly professed their faith through conversion experiences.

By the 1740s, religious fervor, led by itinerant preachers such as George Whitefield, was spreading across New England. Congregationalist preacher and theologian Jonathan Edwards gave his famous sermon, "Sinners in the Hands of an Angry God," a fire and brimstone speech that terrified his audiences. This period of revitalized interest in religion became known as the Great Awakening. To revive interest in religious principles and communities, revivals were held, in which preachers traveled from town to town giving speeches and pressuring entire communities to convert. A Second Great Awakening began around 1795 and peaked in the decades leading up to the Civil War.

By the time Emily Dickinson was born, the religious landscape of America had grown and changed quite significantly. Dissent, revivals, and the formations of new Churches created an era of religious multiplicity. However,

Congregationalists still maintained a stronghold in New England. Emily Dickinson's family was closely tied to the Congregational Church and attended the First Church of Amherst. This orthodox church stayed true to its origins, even when Congregational churches in other areas started abandoning Puritan traditions. Dickinson attended services at the church until sometime in her late twenties. Even when she stopped attending, however, the church's influence was unavoidable. It was a vital part of the Amherst community as a center for church socials, public lectures, and other events. Dickinson grew up hearing her father's stern voice reading passages from the Bible every night, exchanged letters with friends who discussed their conversion experiences, and eventually absorbed and utilized religious tropes in her writing.

Gradually, the society around Emily Dickinson began to change. Up until the Civil War, Amherst was one of the last areas holding onto Puritanism.[2] A major revival swept Amherst in 1845 and then again in 1850, when Dickinson was in her teens. The pressure to publicly profess one's faith as evidence of being "chosen" by God was immense, especially after Dickinson's father and sister underwent conversion experiences.[3] Dickinson, like the minority of people who did not publicly profess their faith, was pressured from all sides; her friends and family members wrote her, concerned that she was not on the path to heaven. With each new convert in her circle, Dickinson had to endure well-meaning but patronizing attempts to save her soul. Between 1840 and 1862, when Dickinson was between the ages of nine and thirty-one, eight revivals passed through Amherst. Despite incalculable pressure from her parents, siblings, peers, and society, she was the only family member who refused to make a public profession of faith.

Dickinson was conflicted about organized religion. As a young adult, she envied the comfort her peers found in a fixed religious system with clear-cut laws, guidelines for behavior, and assurance of heavenly salvation. As an adult, however, she preferred the mortal certainty and mystery of death as well as the ability to define faith and spiritual relationships on her own terms. She believed that the human relationships in *this* life proved more sacred than anything the afterlife might offer. Because no existing religion spoke directly to her needs, Dickinson created her own, blending aspects of Calvinism with her own beliefs. She liberated herself from the church, fostered her own sacred relationships, and achieved moments of grace in the garden instead of the church.

In many ways, Dickinson was a religious rebel. She adopted or rejected aspects of religion as she saw fit, preserving some Puritan traditions when everyone else was becoming more liberal, yet also creating a personal type of religion that projected far beyond the nineteenth century. She was both forward-looking and nostalgic, modern and traditional. Her internal struggle, captured in hundreds of letters and poems, was a spiritual and psychological catharsis. Although Dickinson attempted to connect with others via their religious beliefs, she did not accept their faith as her own and, as a result, found faith in the consistency of her friendships, the evanescence of each moment, and the power of language.

Dickinson was affected by the influences of Puritanism throughout her life. The religion was rooted in the beliefs of simplicity and predestination, as well as the hope for transcendent moments of grace that confirmed one's unity with a sublime God. The Puritan ethics of tradition, social conformity, and constraint directly conflicted with America's progressive, financially driven ambitions. Unwilling to blindly accept either school of thought, Dickinson chose those elements from religion and culture that suited her own beliefs, creating her own view of life centered around the self, home, family, and friends.

Industrialization and the individual

Overall, Emily Dickinson supported the rights of the individual versus the goals of society or tradition. Throughout her life, she questioned authority, whether it was the authority of her father, the church, or society in general. At a time when women were expected to put the comfort and well-being of their husbands and families above themselves, Dickinson always sided with the individual's right to pursue happiness. However, the world she clung to was quickly changing and the emphasis on communal ties was slipping away.

Technological innovation, economic prosperity, and increased immigrant labor led to the emerging industrialization of America. Manufacturing and commerce were thriving: Eli Whitney's cotton gin dramatically increased textile production, newly built railroads facilitated travel and commerce, and the invention of the telegraph connected previously isolated communities. The social and environmental cost of these new technologies, however, was not immediately obvious. Although wealthy Americans could get clothing and other goods faster and cheaper, impoverished Americans and immigrants suffered under abysmal conditions in the factories and along the railroads. Social stratification increased, resulting in conflicts over labor and equality.

The search for more work and a better life also drove growing numbers of Americans from rural communities to urban centers. The Pacific Railroad Act of 1862, which authorized a transcontinental rail line, helped facilitate this population shift. As labor pools left for cities, America's focus on agriculture shifted to urban businesses and corporations. The rise of the market economy also gave power to the American dollar and precipitated the business-driven mindset of competition and materialism. Dickinson echoed the new languages of capitalism and market economy in many of her poems, often for ironic effect. For example, in an 1866 poem she states:

> Myself can read the Telegrams
> A Letter chief to me
> The Stock's advance and Retrograde
> And what the Markets say.
>
> (*P* 493, no. 1089)

Although she could read the public stock market news, for Dickinson, a personal, handwritten letter would always be "chief."

Many people believed the economic changes in the nineteenth century were progressive and exciting. Dickinson, however, remained attached to the quickly fading, quieter, and more contemplative lifestyle. At a time when Americans began to define themselves as members of an expanding nation, Dickinson moved inward, celebrating the individual and interpersonal relationships.

Political culture: expansion and the antebellum period

When Emily Dickinson was born, the United States was a very young country just beginning its quest for expansion. Progress was part of the national vocabulary, closely associated with the desire for additional territory and resources. The country's thirst for land was insatiable.

Congress passed the Indian Removal Act in 1830, which allowed President Jackson to negotiate treaties with Native Americans to exchange land in the Eastern states for land west of the Mississippi River. One of these treaties led to the expulsion of Cherokee Indians from their lands in North Carolina and Georgia. Their 1838 exile to Indian Territory became known as the Trail of Tears. Throughout the 1840s, settlers pressed westward into new territories. On 13 May 1846, Congress declared war on Mexico and acquired lands that eventually became Texas, California, New Mexico, Utah, Arizona, and Nevada. These events were closely tied to Manifest Destiny, the idea that territorial expansion was a religious duty.

Starting in 1846, Mormons began their journey westward to Utah, followed by waves of potential prospectors lured by the 1848 California Gold Rush. To encourage settlement, Congress passed the Homestead Act in 1862. This legislation promised 160 acres of land in the West to any settler who built a house and occupied the land for at least five years.

The US expansion into the West rippled across the country and affected Emily Dickinson's life in several indirect ways. For example, her brother Austin was excited by new opportunities in emerging cities and originally planned to move to another state soon after his marriage to Sue. The thought of Austin moving far away horrified Dickinson and her close-knit family. Edward Dickinson bribed his son to stay, offering to build Austin a home of his own. Although Austin and Sue relented and moved into The Evergreens, several of Dickinson's other friends left for better opportunities in faraway cities. Her beloved Reverend Charles Wadsworth moved to lead a congregation in San Francisco and Samuel Bowles eventually left for Europe. As more and more friends left for better opportunities, Dickinson felt bereft and abandoned.

An even greater fear, however, was slowly building. The anger, rebellion, resentment, and dissent fomenting between the Northern and Southern states was reaching a boiling point with no resolution in sight. As the population wondered how changes would affect racial and state divides, the anticipation of war paralyzed America. In the following poem, Dickinson explores the painful anticipation of the inevitable:

> While we were fearing it, it came –
> But came with less of fear
> Because that fearing it so long
> Had almost made it fair –
>
> There is a Fitting – a Dismay –
> A Fitting – a Despair –
> 'Tis harder knowing it is Due
> Than knowing it is Here.
>
> The Trying on the Utmost
> The Morning it is new
> Is Terribler than wearing it
> A whole existence through.
>
> (*P* 558, no. 1277)

The subject of this poem, "it," may be the Civil War or death itself. Whether focusing on the anxiety surrounding impending war or death, the poem describes the paradox of how "knowing it is Due" is actually "harder" than the experience itself. In the second stanza, Dickinson puns on the word "Fitting" both as a noun, or the experience of meeting with a tailor for clothing measurements, and as an adjective, meaning something that perfectly describes a person or thing. As garments, Dismay and Despair are fitted to the speaker just as the speaker becomes adjusted to them. They are clothes that can be tried on briefly or worn for a lifetime, a "whole existence through." In the third stanza, the speaker shifts from fearing the inevitable to "wearing it" or accepting it. Once the speaker accepts the inevitability of war or death, the anticipation becomes bearable. However, the "Morning it is new" becomes more terrible in comparison.

The elegant ambivalence of the poem describes America's antebellum era, which was marked by anxiety and terror over if and when the war would begin, how it would affect everyday life, and what the outcome would be for slaves, freed slaves, Northerners, and Southerners alike. Dickinson understood that the terror of the unknown could be more frightening than the event itself. Because she embraced death and accepted it as a common event that all mortals would share, she did not waste energy on fearing and avoiding it. However, the acceptance of a natural death was not the same as the acceptance of death in war. These were themes that she continued to explore in the years leading up to and including the Civil War.

Social movements: Abolition and women's rights

Although there were groups opposed to slavery as early as the founding of the Republic, slavery was legal in almost all of the states. The word "slavery" was not used in the Constitution; however, the document had several provisions that accommodated slavery. Massachusetts was the first state to formally abolish slavery, followed by all of the states in the North by 1830. Then an increased sense of mission infused the abolitionist movement. Organizers such as white activist William Lloyd Garrison and former slave Frederick Douglass demanded immediate emancipation for black people.

Abolitionism and religion were also closely aligned, with many Quakers and converts from the Second Great Awakening joining the movement. Because of their religious beliefs, many Northerners believed that all people, regardless of race, were children of God, and therefore slavery should be prohibited. Many Southerners, however, also believed that religion supported their side, stating that slavery was not explicitly prohibited in any of the Bible's Scriptures.

In the Southern states, economy, culture, tradition, and social beliefs were tightly interwoven with issues of slavery. The ownership of slaves was part and parcel of the Southern economy. As time progressed, the institution became connected with the idea of states' rights. Believing in the ultimate supremacy of the states' individual rights to govern themselves, Southerners felt the abolitionist movement was an affront to their rights.

Many brave Americans who opposed slavery supported the Underground Railroad, a secret network that helped Southern slaves escape to Free states in the North and Canada. The Fugitive Slave Law of 1850, however, was enacted in order to counteract the Underground Railroad. This law stated that escaped slaves caught in the North would have to be returned to slaveholders in the South. Northerners viewed this law as an extreme intrusion of slavery into their borders, and felt an even greater need to fight slavery. However, some Northerners supported the law, angering many abolitionists. When Northern politician Daniel Webster spoke out in support of the law, many abolitionists felt betrayed.

Emily Dickinson followed all of these events in the newspapers and through her father. For example, while her father was at a national Whig convention in 1852, Dickinson wrote, "Why cant I be a Delegate to the great Whig Convention? – dont I know all about Daniel Webster, and the Tariff, and the Law?" (*L* 212, no. 94). Many of Dickinson's most influential friends were abolitionists. Thomas Wentworth Higginson, for example, traveled through the South and was one of the first to collect slave spirituals and ballads.[4] He was a fervent abolitionist and supported John Brown's Raid at Harper's Ferry, a violent and controversial raid on an ammunition storehouse in Virginia that occurred on 16 October 1859. By 1860, the polarizing beliefs of the North and South had reached a fever pitch. With South Carolina's 20 December secession from the Union, Americans knew that war was imminent.

Meanwhile, a rebellion that paralleled the abolitionist struggle was taking place. As Americans argued about individual rights and personhood, women began to clamor for rights of their own. When Dickinson was seventeen, the first women's rights convention was held in Seneca Falls, New York, about 300 miles away from Amherst.[5] The 1848 Seneca Falls Convention was a landmark event in American feminist history. Although the teenaged Dickinson probably did not consider herself connected to the Seneca Falls women, her developing thoughts about independence, education for women, and sisterhood were in line with theirs. Later in life, Dickinson befriended Samuel Bowles, Helen Hunt Jackson, and Thomas Wentworth Higginson, three people who supported women's writing and shared liberal views about women's rights.[6]

Dickinson knew that suffragists and abolitionists were working together to accomplish similar goals: increased civil rights and liberties for all people. She also followed the advancements in both causes through her father's political connections and Sue's willingness to host abolitionists and suffragists at The Evergreens. For example, both Harriet Beecher Stowe, author of *Uncle Tom's Cabin*, and Wendell Phillips, a prominent abolitionist and suffragist, stayed at

The Evergreens. Both causes were obviously important issues for the Dickinson families.

Philosophical reactions: Transcendentalism

In addition to the religious, cultural, and political events occurring during Dickinson's lifetime, philosophical movements shaped her writing as well. Perhaps one of the most important movements connected to Dickinson was Transcendentalism. This movement praised humankind's ability to transcend the mortal world through reflection, intuition, and an openness to nature. The movement included many writers, most notably Ralph Waldo Emerson, Henry David Thoreau, and Walt Whitman. They praised individualism, self-reliance, and racial and sexual equality. One of their most heretical beliefs was that an individual could attain sublime moments of grace by studying nature and becoming the mortal embodiment of God. The Transcendentalists believed that individuals could have a direct relationship with God without having to go through middlemen such as ministers or religious teachers.

Transcendentalism began as a religious movement within the Unitarian Church. Unlike the Puritans, who believed in original sin, a hostile world, and a predestined universe, the Unitarians believed that the world was basically good and that people could attain salvation through good works. Many Transcendentalists were practicing or former Unitarian ministers, including Emerson and Theodore Parker.

As the movement grew, it responded to the major national preoccupations of expansionism, industrialization, Abolition, women's rights, and the Civil War. Like Dickinson, the Transcendentalists believed that the country's new focus on profit was replacing personal craftsmanship and alienating people from their communities and natural surroundings. Transcendentalists sought to restore the vital connection between nature, people, and God.

Although not considered a Transcendentalist, Emily Dickinson was closely aligned with the movement. She owned, read, and quoted books by Emerson, who stayed with Austin and Sue Dickinson at The Evergreens in 1857 and again in 1865.[7] Although it is not known if Dickinson saw Emerson during this time, she would have heard about his visit.

Emerson claimed that the individual's likeness to God lies in internal powers rather than knowledge of church doctrine or adherence to clerical rituals. Replacing the logic and reason of doctrine with intuition, insight, and sentiment, Emerson emphasized the visceral and emotional components of spirituality over the strictly intellectual approach of the church. Emerson also insisted that individuals achieve perfection through self-reliance, a way to achieve sublime spirituality. For Emerson and later Transcendentalists, it was not God who would save, but virtue itself; it was not knowledge or faith in God's teachings, but the enactment or embodiment of virtues that restored man's purity.

The worldview Dickinson constructs in her poetry reflects what might be called a Transcendental legacy in antebellum American letters. In her resistance to organized religion and inherited doctrines, her willingness to replace God with people as a subject of devotion and praise, and her belief in the power of human consciousness to discover eternal truths in the natural world, Dickinson injects the basic tenets of Transcendentalism into her poetry.

Both Emily Dickinson and the Transcendentalists grew weary of church dogma and sought to break away from organized religion. For example, Dickinson wrote, "Mr S. preached in our church last Sabbath upon 'predestination,' but I do not respect 'doctrines,' and did not listen to him" (*L* 346, no. 200). She rejected predestination, refused to attend church, and rebelled against a particularly strong history of religion and tradition. If Puritanism sought to limit the barriers between God and humanity by restructuring the clergy's role in religious experience, Transcendentalists like Emerson took Puritanism to the extreme by removing doctrinal religion entirely in the quest for spiritual fulfillment.

Dickinson's poetry embodies her tacit agreement with Emerson about the traditions of poetry and religion. She abandoned standard meter and rhyme, threw conventional grammar out the window, and forced her readers to work to understand her meaning. The traditional structures of poetry were incapable of conveying the ideas she wanted to express. Her declaration to Thomas Wentworth Higginson that "while my thought is undressed – I can make the distinction, but when I put them in the Gown – they look alike, and numb," demonstrates her need for raw, unadorned thought rather than traditional words confined in "Gown" (*L* 404, no. 261).

Like the Transcendentalists, Dickinson's abandonment of the church did not mean a relinquishment of spiritual discovery. Instead, it allowed a heightened possibility for personal revelation. Heaven, for Dickinson, was not the otherworldly destination of Christian scripture, but something that could be attained in the present. Dickinson's vision of an earthly heaven resembled William Ellery Channing's notion of human perfectibility; both contradicted traditional teachings while embracing some ultimate aims of Christianity – virtuous living, spiritual enlightenment, solemn introspection, and admiration of God. Dickinson, like Channing and the Transcendentalists, departed from Christianity in her belief that faith in humankind, and not an exclusive faith in God, will raise the common individual's physical and spiritual well-being.

Dickinson's assertion that the self shall "Suffice . . . for a Crowd" sounds remarkably similar to Emerson's claim in "Self-Reliance" that "every true man is a cause, a country, and an age."[8] Dickinson read Emerson's book *Representative Men* and called it "a little Granite Book you can lean upon" (*L* 569, no. 481).

Although Dickinson shared Transcendental beliefs with Emerson, Thoreau, and others, and experimented with words in a very Whitman-like fashion, it is important to recognize differences between Dickinson and her contemporaries. One of the key differences is her use of "circumference." Emerson used the term to describe the ideals outside of the individual that, although unattainable, should still be goals. Dickinson, however, believed that "circumference" was not only attainable, but already a part of everyday experience.

Dickinson wanted to determine the edges of experience, the periphery or circumference, rather than focus on the center. Writing to Higginson in 1862, she declares, "My Business is Circumference" (*L* 412, no. 268). She also utilized the term in poems, noting "When Cogs – stop – that's Circumference" (*P* 313, no. 633). Her commitment to circumference – embracing life with the most complete and comprehensive perspective – shows her belief that people can be divine and yet human, attached to nature and God, but not necessarily tethered to religion.

The Civil War

The four-year period of the Civil War (1861–5) was the bloodiest era America had yet seen. It was also the most prolific time of Emily Dickinson's writing. Suddenly the clashes between individual and society, agrarian and industrial, black and white, and North and South came to a head. The severity of the war put Dickinson into a brand new existential challenge, one that had no previous models. The new advances in weapon technology, including the Gatling gun (a rapid-repeating firearm) and the Minié ball (a bullet that allowed rapid muzzle-loading of rifles), combined with the sheer scale of the war, forced Dickinson to grapple with issues of liberty, life, and death in a way she never had before.[9]

Edward Dickinson's involvement in politics and support of the Northern war effort meant that his family was kept abreast of evolving news about the war.[10] Dickinson's brother Austin avoided conscription by paying $500 for an Irish laborer to join the Union army in his stead. Although Austin was spared, Dickinson knew friends and relatives who were not as fortunate. In March of 1862, Dickinson was devastated by the death of Lieutenant Frazar Stearns, son of Amherst College's President and friend of Austin. In a letter to her Norcross cousins, Dickinson describes "brave Frazer":

"killed at Newbern," darlings. His big heart shot away by a "minie ball."

I had read of those – I didn't think that Frazer would carry one to Eden with him. Just as he fell, in his soldier's cap, with his sword at his side, Frazer rode through Amherst. Classmates to the right of him, and classmates to the left of him, to guard his narrow face! He fell by the side of Professor Clark, his superior officer – lived ten minutes in a soldier's arms, asked twice for water – murmured just, "My God!" and passed! . . . They tell that Colonel Clark cried like a little child . . . and could hardly resume his post. They loved each other very much.

(*L* 397–8, no. 255)

Although Dickinson states that she "had read" about the new "minie ball," the technology takes on a new, horribly personal meaning when it is attached to the death of a friend. While describing the senseless tragedy of Stearns' death, Dickinson references a famous 1854 poem by Alfred, Lord Tennyson. "The Charge of the Light Brigade" dramatized the massacre of British cavalrymen during the Crimean War. Dickinson echoes the poem's hypnotic lines, "Cannon to right of them, / Cannon to left of them, / Cannon in front of them," with her version, "Classmates to the right of him, and classmates to the left of him."[11] By doing so, Dickinson aligns her own beliefs about the Civil War with Tennyson's beliefs about the futile and senseless deaths of the Crimean War.

Dickinson does not spare her cousins the tragic details: because Stearns' "narrow face" had been exposed and his "big heart shot away," his body was not fit for viewing. "Nobody here could look on Frazer – not even his father. The doctors would not allow it," she notes (*L* 398, no. 25). Stearns' death also inspired an elegy:

> It feels a shame to be Alive –
> When Men so brave – are dead –
> One envies the Distinguished Dust –
> Permitted – such a Head –
>
> The Stone – that tells defending Whom
> This Spartan put away
> What little of Him we – possessed
> In Pawn for Liberty –
>
> The price is great – Sublimely paid –
> Do we deserve – a Thing –
> That lives – like Dollars – must be piled
> Before we may obtain?

> Are we that wait – sufficient worth –
> That such Enormous Pearl
> As life – dissolved be – for Us –
> In Battle's – horrid Bowl?
>
> It may be – a Renown to live –
> I think the Man who die –
> Those unsustained – Saviors –
> Present Divinity –   (*P* 213, no. 444)

In the poem, Dickinson contrasts her guilt at living when "Men so brave" as Stearns are dying. However, just as she elevates the dying soldier and honors his valor, she questions whether the reason – war – is worth the price of life. "The price is great" she warns, once again using language from the world of economics and industrialization, then shows that the only way this price can be paid is "Sublimely," or in an intangible way that most cannot understand. She further asks, does society deserve liberty if it comes at the cost of so many lives? Dickinson's critique of material wealth is also subtle: the soldiers' bodies are stacked "like Dollars" and their lives are an "Enormous Pearl" that is "dissolved" by war. For Dickinson, the soldiers are mere game pieces who are used to lose or win victories. Clearly, Dickinson is torn between paying tribute to the heroic efforts of friends such as Stearns and drawing attention to the utter waste of their deaths.

At first glance, Dickinson's poems written during the Civil War do not appear to be "war" poems. However, careful reading shows that several of her poems are in fact closely connected to the events of the war. Dickinson did not live in a self-sealed bubble; she isolated her physical body but allowed her intellect and imagination to trespass all boundaries. Like others of her era, Dickinson experienced the Civil War as the central event of her life that colored everything that followed.

Higginson's connections to the Civil War are particularly important when examining the war's effect on Dickinson. Higginson was a colonel for the First South Carolina Volunteers, the first regiment of black soldiers (freed slaves) in the Civil War. Dickinson wrote to Higginson after he was injured in battle: "Dear friend, Are you in danger – I did not know that you were hurt. Will you tell me more? . . . I am surprised and anxious" (*L* 431, no. 290).

In competitions and war, victory is all that matters. To lose is to show weakness, failure, and despair, but to win is to exhibit strength, success, and great satisfaction. Dickinson, however, saw an essential paradox within the dichotomies of winning and losing:

Success is counted sweetest
By those who ne'er succeed.
To comprehend a nectar
Requires sorest need.

Not one of all the purple Host
Who took the Flag today
Can tell the definition
So clear of Victory

As he defeated – dying –
On whose forbidden ear
The distant strains of triumph
Burst agonized and clear!

(*P* 35, no. 67)

According to Dickinson, no one understands what winning means more than those who have lost. Whereas the victor understands only one side, the loser comprehends both. Knowing the pain of losing and imagining the thrill of succeeding, the defeated side suffers from an intensely emotional, holistic understanding of their war experience.

Perhaps the Civil War's strongest impact upon Dickinson can be seen in her use of martial imagery. She internalized the Civil War: the conflict of religious beliefs, anger over authority, suppression of individual rights and liberties, and the reality of death. She also viewed the war as an externalization of her own battle between autonomy and submission. The nation's Civil War was a macrocosm of the civil war Dickinson waged inside herself. She uses the images of war, battle, weaponry, and death in her most famous poem from 1863:

My Life had stood – a Loaded Gun –
In Corners – till a Day
The Owner passed – identified
And carried Me away –

And now We roam in Sovereign Woods –
And now We hunt the Doe –
And every time I speak for Him –
The Mountains straight reply –

And do I smile, such cordial light
Upon the Valley glow –
It is as a Vesuvian face
Had let its pleasure through –

And when at Night – Our good Day done –
I guard My Master's Head –
'Tis better than the Eider-Duck's
Deep Pillow – to have shared –

To foe of His – I'm deadly foe –
None stir the second time –
On whom I lay a Yellow Eye –
Or an emphatic Thumb –

Though I than He – may longer live
He longer must – than I –
For I have but the power to kill,
Without – the power to die –

(*P* 369–70, no. 754)

In this poem, the speaker's life is fraught with possibility – a "Loaded Gun" is full of dangerous potential. It can be used for hunting animals for food, killing people in war, or even as a tool for suicide. The gun is ready but the poem's speaker must decide if, and when, to shoot, who will pull the trigger, and what will be caught in the fire.

Dickinson's ambiguous personal pronouns, "Me," "We" and "Him," invite the reader to delve into the poem and supply the situation. In many ways, the poem's refusal to be easily translated or pinned to a single interpretation opens it to successive generations of readers. Critics have focused on the poem's use of gender ("Him," "My Master," the female deer), politics (the "Sovereign" woods), religion ("Him" as God, "Sovereign," the echo from the mountains), and martial imagery (the gun, the ricochet, "power to kill"). The speaker's life is a gun standing in a corner, a tool waiting for action. Although many critics interpret the poem's hunter to be the male force that takes hold of Dickinson's life, it could just as well be a different aspect of her own psyche. Her life may be the gun, but what she decides to do with it is her own choice. The poem vacillates between the speaker's autonomy as a powerful weapon and the speaker's submission to an "Owner." One reading of the poem considers the act of writing as the gun itself. Dickinson's words are certainly "loaded" and, like the gun itself, have the potential for immortality.

"There's the Battle of Burgoyne – / Over, every day," writes Dickinson in a poem from 1870 (*P* 522, no. 1174). Although referencing a specific battle from the Revolutionary War, these lines show that battles and wars occur on a personal level every day. There are battles to define the self and its position

in the world, battles against authorities that seek to curb individual expression, battles against unjust social practices, and the final battle against the
lifelong foe, death. Dickinson was a Civil War poet whose battlefront was the
printed page; as she proclaimed, "My Wars are laid away in Books" (*P* 645,
no. 1549).

Chapter 3

Works

Sweeping with many-colored brooms: the influence
   of the domestic *51*
Blasphemous devotion: biblical allusion in the poems and letters *58*
"Easy, quite, to love": friendship and love in Dickinson's life
   and works *70*
"The Heaven – below": nature poems *86*
"A Riddle, at the last": death and immortality *97*

Complex, confusing, provocative, intimidating, profound, unorthodox: these are some of the words that describe the work of Emily Dickinson. No introduction to Dickinson's work is more appropriate than her own definition of poetry as recorded by Thomas Wentworth Higginson: "If I read a book [and] it makes my whole body so cold no fire ever can warm me I know *that* is poetry. If I feel physically as if the top of my head were taken off, I know *that* is poetry. These are the only way I know it. Is there any other way" (*L* 473–4, no. 342a). This visceral, concrete, and highly personal definition of poetry is the most fitting way to view Dickinson's own work. Whether a poem is true "poetry" does not depend for Dickinson on its use of meter, rhyme, stanzas, or line length, but on the almost physical sensation created in the reader by the poem's words, the arctic chill in the marrow of the bones or the stunning blow to the mind that the reader experiences in the act of reading. Dickinson's interest in creating such a sensation makes her poetry unorthodox and difficult to understand. Often abandoning conventional poetic standards, Dickinson chose her words for the feeling they create, for their ability to awaken in the reader a specific emotion at the moment described. However, as a result, many readers approaching Dickinson for the first time find themselves overwhelmed and perplexed by her work. In fact, some do not teach Dickinson's work because her syntax is often abstruse and puzzling. However, these are the very qualities that make Dickinson's groundbreaking poetry rewarding. Her letters and poems provide fresh ways to investigate and understand the emotional, intellectual, and psychological nature of humanity.

Poetry enabled Dickinson to achieve an equilibrium between personal autonomy and emotional dependence. Her comprehensive vision and her commitment to "circumference," or the inner and outer experiences that drive the individual, allowed her to accept and celebrate life despite its dualistic inevitabilities of grief and joy, despair and hope. Dickinson sought connecting patterns in life rather than metaphysical explanations. Less concerned with what *should be* than with what *was*, she focused her energy on the concrete details of the present moment. Through her writing, Dickinson expresses anxiety about the uncertainty of life while paradoxically stressing the value and profound importance of life's journey. Her moral and artistic vision was essentially holistic, generative, and comprehensive rather than linear, compartmentalized, and categorical. Dualism, contradiction, and oxymoron all played critical roles in Dickinson's life and works. Rejecting the male-centered Victorian worldview that divided flesh and spirit and seeking to explain away life's contradictions, Emily Dickinson fostered a more feminine vision of the world. "Instead of willful individualism and an effort to transcend the temporal world, Dickinson evolved a nurturing vision based on a cyclical flux of interconnected life forms."[1] Dickinson rejected standard dualisms that divided the world into flesh and spirit, saved and damned, mortal and immortal. She represents Emerson's "transparent eyeball" – that is, someone who embodies life's fullness and complexity with complete objectivity – and acts as a guide to reveal the world in its harmoniously disparate fullness.

In order to understand life and the complex intricacy of her psyche, Dickinson required solitude; at the same time, she craved closeness and communion with those she loved. Hers was a delicate balancing act: to remain both isolated and connected, individual but intimately involved with others. Poetry gave Dickinson the medium for exploring such tensions. Her poetic style attempts to capture the conflicts and emotions of the moment; her idiosyncrasies result from her attempt to find an appropriate form "for representing an untethered inner life."[2]

Dickinson defied all poetic rules and as a result created inventive poems that allowed her to capture thoughts and emotions in dramatic, though often enigmatic, fashion. The Dickinson trademark – the dash – breaks lines apart, forcing the reader to pause and reconsider and providing a visible, physical space for thought. The dashes often invite the reader to fill in the blanks. Dickinson's unconventional use of punctuation, especially the dash, serves almost as a kind of musical notation that guides the rhythm of the lines. Her slant rhymes and strange syntax help create a comprehensive vision of a world that defies regularization, predictability, and order. Instead of following poetic conventions, Dickinson often purposely avoids regularizing her verse. For example, in the final line of "If I'm lost – now," Dickinson purposely ignores using an easy rhyme ("thee") as the final word of the poem:

> I'm banished – now – you know it –
> How foreign that can be –
> You'll know – Sir – when the Savior's face
> Turns so – away from you –
>
> (*P* 117, no. 256)

The final "you" of the poem jars the reader's ears, suddenly and forcibly placing the reader in the position of distance and abandonment from God. Dickinson's irregularity thus serves a poetic purpose. She often inverted language, omitted auxiliary verbs, used adjectives, verbs, and adverbs as nouns, and concluded sentences or clauses with verbs in order to disrupt the balance of her lines and to create abrupt and striking sensations in the reader. That which makes readers feel uncomfortable – Dickinson's use of nouns as verbs, slant rhymes, perplexing meter, ambiguous speakers – works metaphorically to convey the experience of chaos. "[T]he inherent chaos of sense perception," a perception to which Dickinson was committed, is conveyed in the very language and rhythms of Dickinson's poems; "[d]isorder, therefore, is conveyed in Dickinson's poetry not only imagistically and thematically. It is represented linguistically and visually as well."[3] Embracing the disjunction and contradiction that life involves, Dickinson seeks to re-create the unpredictable and often jarring rhythms of life.

Dickinson's unusual poetic style was a rebellion against the Victorian tendency to explain and narrow the world. She distrusted attempts to create easy explanations for the various experiences of life. Dickinson found wholeness, not by excising the harsh realities of life and looking to a future of uniform happiness, but by accepting life's jarring disjunctions as well as its pleasures. The hymn writer Isaac Watts (1674–1748) was for Dickinson the epitome of regularity and simplistic religious explanations of the world. Dickinson's poetic irregularity was a direct response to Watts' strict 4-3-4-3 meters and heavily rhymed lines. She mocked such predictable and, sometimes, leaden hymns by using their meter as the bass for her own more complicated jazz style.[4] The following hymn demonstrates Watts' "steady cadences and inexorable rhymes"[5]:

> God of the Seas, thy thundering Voice
> Makes all the roaring Waves rejoice,
> And one soft Word of thy Command
> Can sink them silent in the Sand.
> If but a Moses wave thy Rod,
> The Sea Divides and owns its God;

The stormy Floods their maker knew,
And let his chosen Armies thro!

The Scaly Flocks amidst the Sea
To thee their Lord a Tribute pay;
The meanest Fish that swims the Flood
Leaps up, and means a Praise to God.[6]

The hammering regularity of Watts' trite lines extolling God's control over the seas, as demonstrated in the parting of the Red Sea (Exodus 14), reads very differently than Dickinson's satiric version of the story:

"Red Sea," indeed! Talk not to me
Of purple Pharaoh –
I have a Navy in the West
Would pierce his Columns thro' –
Guileless, yet of such Glory fine
That all along the Line
Is it, or is it not, Marine –
Is it, or not, divine –
The Eye inquires with a sigh
That Earth sh'd be so big –
What Exultation in the Woe –
What Wine in the fatigue!
(*P* 673, no. 1642)

Dickinson's slant rhymes and colloquial language complement her satiric reading of the biblical narrative of judgment. Her project, so different from Watts', requires a more rebellious, less regular poetic form. Likewise, Watts' "Christ Jesus, the Lamb of God" displays his strict adherence to meter and emphasis on rhyme. Watts uses impeccable scansion, rhyme, and language to describe heavenly perfection:

Let all that dwell above the sky,
And Air, and Earth, and Seas
Conspire to lift thy Glory high,
And speak thine endless Praise.

The whole Creation join in one,
To bless the Sacred Name
Of him that sits upon the Throne,
And to adore the Lamb.[7]

Rather than mimic Watts' style, Dickinson mocks his simplistic worldview that fails to recognize this world's many perfections:

> Who has not found the Heaven – below –
> Will fail of it above –
> For Angels rent the House next ours,
> Where we remove –   (*P* 644, no. 1544)

By replacing the reassuring, rhythmic pace of Watts' hymn with jerky, halting disjunction, Dickinson attacks the limited message of Watts' hymn. Whereas Watts celebrates the afterlife in a very rigid poetic manner, Dickinson's staccato praise of this world suggests a worldview that embraces all aspects of reality rather than looking forward to a heaven with no complexities.

Dickinson's commitment to the full range of life's experiences makes her poetic explorations of the human soul both powerful and dangerous. Abandoning herself to the present emotion provided Dickinson with moments of ecstasy but also left her on the verge of chaotic breakdown at times. Her vision of the universe became a dangerous balancing act. The precariousness of her position and the anxiety she felt are obvious in "I stepped from Plank to Plank":

> I stepped from Plank to Plank
> A slow and cautious way
> The Stars about my Head I felt
> About my Feet the Sea.
>
> I knew not but the next
> Would be my final inch –
> This gave me that precarious Gait
> Some call Experience.
>
> (*P* 416–17, no. 875)

For Dickinson, each moment is a dangerous balancing between experiencing ecstatic, starry visions and falling into the swirling chaos of life. Her gait is halting and precarious because a false step means chaos and destruction. Despite the perilous nature of her approach, Dickinson still remains connected to her actual experience. Her frank bravery and commitment to experience allow Dickinson to continue, despite the dangers: "Although the stars whirl around her head, and the sea swirls at her feet, she remains grounded, however tentatively, in the moment."[8] Dickinson's fear of the unknown does not restrain her; rather, it encourages her to discover what experience will be next. Despite some trepidation, she courageously marches onward in her efforts to experience life.

In her poetry, Dickinson often perches on the razor's edge between absolute chaos and transcendent wisdom. Plunging into the depths of the mind can be a dangerous task. Her grasp of reason sometimes seems to falter when she identifies too closely with despair or grief. These explorations reveal dangers within the psyche:

> One need not be a Chamber – to be Haunted –
> One need not be a House –
> The Brain has Corridors – surpassing
> Material Place –
>
> Far safer, of a Midnight Meeting
> External Ghost
> Than its interior Confronting –
> That Cooler Host.
>
> Far safer, through an Abbey gallop,
> The Stones a'chase –
> Than Unarmed, one's a'self encounter –
> In lonesome Place –
>
> Ourself behind ourself, concealed –
> Should startle most –
> Assassin hid in our Apartment
> Be Horror's least.
>
> The Body – borrows a Revolver –
> He bolts the Door –
> O'erlooking a superior spectre –
> Or More –   (*P* 333, no. 670)

Dickinson explores the possibility of being haunted by one's own mind, past, or feelings. Her own mind can become the haunting "spectre" that threatens to kill or endangers her body's well-being. The chaotic depths of the mind hold dangerous secrets that seem ready to kill the self. The chaotic labyrinths in the mind have the ability to destroy, but Dickinson boldly continues to explore them.

  Dickinson was committed to embracing life and humanity in all its chaotic fullness and darkness. She accepted death as part of life. Such acceptance led to an even deeper reverence for life. With no certainty of an afterlife, Dickinson chooses to treasure this life's potential to its fullest:

> To be alive – is Power –
> Existence – in itself –
> Without a further function –
> Omnipotence – Enough –

> To be alive – and Will!
> 'Tis able as a God –
> The Maker – of Ourselves – be what –
> Such being Finitude!
>
> (*P* 335–6, no. 677)

To Dickinson, daily life is a powerful gift and the joy she finds in that fleeting moment is "Enough." Every individual is a "God" who shapes life and acts as "The Maker – of Ourselves." "This poem contains the kernel of Dickinson's cosmology: life as an end in itself is inherently powerful, while life dedicated to control can create the illusion of omnipotence but ultimately exposes the limitations of human will."[9] "Forever is composed of Nows" (*P* 307, no. 624). Rather than being controlled by the hopes of an afterlife, Dickinson shapes her own existence through the enjoyment of each of life's infinite moments. The great responsibility of living life in the moment sometimes weighs on Dickinson, but ultimately she triumphs in the infinite possibilities it offers:

> I am afraid to own a Body –
> I am afraid to own a Soul –
> Profound – precarious Property –
> Possession, not optional –
>
> Double Estate – entailed at pleasure
> Upon an unsuspecting Heir –
> Duke in a moment of Deathlessness
> And God, for a Frontier.
>
> (*P* 493–4, no. 1090)

While the weighty responsibility of life makes Dickinson at times "afraid to own a Body" and "a Soul," this "Double Estate," while it is a precarious possession, is also a wonderful gift. To own one's body and soul is to be the "Duke" of each precious moment, moments which are "deathless" in the infinity of possibility they offer. To own one's soul is to have "God," the godlike reaches of the mind and soul, for one's "Frontier" as well as to be God over the "Frontier" of one's life journey, a frontier that offers beautiful and dangerous landscapes for exploration. Dickinson's project then is to explore fully the frontiers of life and of the mind that are given her for this brief infinity that is her earthly existence. These opportunities provide enough power and omnipotence without the necessity of an afterlife. The daily experiences of life, the quotidian details that surrounded her were enough. Dickinson never took the quotidian for granted. She paid close attention to everything around her, from the spider webs in the kitchen to the mourners in the town cemetery. The themes that predominantly occupied her thoughts included the domestic realm and the joy of solitude, the infinite value of friendship, the beauty of nature, and the undeniable yet paradoxically reassuring fact of mortality.

Dickinson redefined poetry with her shrewd insight, her unorthodox writing style, and her courageous creativity in pursuit of each living moment. Using words and punctuation as symbols for her consciousness, Dickinson voiced the chaotic transcendence of her intellectual and life experience. Readers tend to approach Dickinson's poetry much the same way Dickinson approached life; feeling overwhelmed, fearful, and excited about the ensuing moment, they find great satisfaction in persevering.

Of course, no introduction to Emily Dickinson's works would be complete without a discussion of her letters, which are sometimes considered even more fascinating than her poems. Because she chose not to formally publish, Dickinson used her letters to circulate poetry among her friends. Dickinson is unusual among American poets because of her reliance upon letters as a place to create, refine, circulate, and "publish" poems. In fact, to understand her work as a poet, one must understand her work as a correspondent. In her letters, Dickinson consoled grieving friends, celebrated births and marriages, expressed longing for absent friends and lovers, and engaged in deep discussions about the nature of art, religion, and death. As she grew older and saw fewer and fewer people in person, Dickinson relied upon letters to be her primary connection to the outside world.

As an upper-class nineteenth-century New England woman, Emily Dickinson was immersed in epistolary culture. Letter-writing was not only an acceptable occupation for women, but also one that was heavily encouraged by society. There were several handbooks and etiquette guides to teach women the correct way to write letters. However, just as Dickinson bent the forms of traditionally accepted poetry, she also stretched the limits of her letters. An 1850 letter to Jane Humphrey shows the complex ways that Dickinson approached letter-writing:

> I have written you a great many letters since you left me – not the kind of letters that go in post-offices – and ride in mail-bags – but queer – little silent ones – very full of affection – and full of confidence – but wanting in proof to you – therefore not valid – somehow you will not answer them – and you *would* paper, and ink letters – I will try one of those – tho' not half so precious as the other kind. I have written *those* at night – when the rest of the world were at sleep – when only God came between us – and no one else might hear. No need of shutting the door – . . . for night held them fast in his arms that they could not interfere – and his arms are brawny and strong. Sometimes I did'nt know but you were awake – and I hoped you wrote with that spirit pen – and on sheets from out the sky. (*L* 81, no. 30)

Here, Dickinson describes the letters she writes in her thoughts, the "queer" intangible letters that travel by love or telepathy rather than postman. Dickinson acknowledges that these letters (perhaps like her own poems) are "not valid" because they are not written in the traditional form. However, she challenges the reader to accept letters written by "spirit pen" because they are like prayer – precious, heartfelt, and composed at night while everyone else sleeps. This is an example of how Dickinson's letters were more than just a means to convey information. They became artistic and literary texts in their own right.

Emily Dickinson's letters were object lessons, gifts, and multimedia art presentations. They were carefully considered and wrought, sometimes demanding, often playful. Even the simple act of sending food next door to The Evergreens was an occasion for wit, consideration, and love. For example, she once sent roasting chickens to Austin and Sue with a note that read, "Brother, Sister, Ned. Enclosed please find the Birds which do not go South" (*L* 879, no. 997). Her letters were accompanied by poems, sketches, pencil stubs, flowers, food, fruits, and once even a cricket, which appropriately accompanied a poem titled "My Cricket."[10] She used different types of paper for different people and occasions. For example, she wrote on graph paper, scrap paper, and embossed and gilt-trimmed stationery, "in effect dressing her texts like a gift edition of poetry or a deluxe edition of biblical scripture."[11]

Her letters of sympathy and condolence are an important facet of Dickinson's writing. Dickinson's preoccupation with the funeral services she could see from her window did not make her morbid or unusual. During this era, child mortality rates were high, life expectancy was low, and medical practices were much more primitive than they are today. The most common ailment of the time, consumption, earned its name because its victims coughed blood and rapidly lost weight as if they were being consumed from the inside out. Death was not sanitized or hidden – it was often graphic and public. A woman of Dickinson's position in society would not only know many people who suffered and died from tuberculosis, but would also be expected to offer sympathy and send her condolences each time someone died. Writers in the mid-1800s, including Walt Whitman and Henry James, became experts at crafting condolence letters partially because they had so many to write. As any person who has had to write a condolence letter knows, extending sympathy toward a grieving parent, sibling, or spouse is extremely difficult. For Dickinson, the task was more than a dreaded responsibility; it was a chance to help heal someone's wounds with her words.

For example, in 1878, after the death of Samuel Bowles, Dickinson discreetly and tenderly wrote to Maria Whitney, who was his mistress. Both Dickinson and Whitney secretly held great affection, most likely love, for Bowles. Dickinson knew that Whitney could not grieve publicly as a widow for someone else's husband, but would nonetheless feel the anguish of a bereft wife. When writing to grieving friends, Dickinson did not "try to dilute their pain with sentimental clichés about a happier afterlife" but instead "gave them solace based on her own experience of loss."[12] She wrote to Maria Whitney, "I have thought of you often since the darkness, – though we cannot assist another's night" (*L* 602, no. 537). Dickinson was a great comfort to the recipients of her letters. She realized that "to accept the connection between life and death is to grow as a person; to deny it is to bury a part of oneself in repression and denial."[13]

While many of Dickinson's letters conveyed sympathy and condolence and many others were expressions of love and friendship, her letters often indicated hurt and inspired guilt. She wrote letters that could be "a kind of snakebite in words, both professing affection and making a winding and wounding display of unconcern."[14] Strong expressions of love gave way at times to deep anger for an often imagined wrong. Dickinson's letters thus reveal much to the reader about her complex relationships with others.

A key trait linking Dickinson's letters to her poetry is the use of personas. Although many of Dickinson's poems are written in the first person, the identity of the speaker frequently changes. Readers should be careful not to automatically assume that a first person poem is about Dickinson herself, although it is tempting to do so. Dickinson constantly played with the boundaries of her identity and this is evident in the body of her letters. The names she used to identify herself inside letters, or the names she used to sign the letters at the end, include "Emilie," "Judah," "Phaeton," "Brooks of Sheffield," "Cole," "Samuel Nash," "Antony," and "Uncle Emily." She can assume the role of man or woman, Biblical foe or Shakespearean hero, all by the choice of persona.

Perhaps the most important Dickinson letters were those she wrote to Thomas Wentworth Higginson. Her first letter to Higginson, written on 15 April 1862, reads:

> Mr. Higginson,
> Are you too deeply occupied to say if my Verse is alive?
> The Mind is so near itself – it cannot see, distinctly – and I have none to ask –
> Should you think it breathed – and had you the leisure to tell me, I should feel quick gratitude –
> If I make the mistake – that you dared to tell me – would give me sincerer honor – toward you –
> I enclose my name – asking you, if you please – Sir – to tell me what is true?
> That you will not betray me – it is needless to ask – since Honor is it's own pawn – (*L* 403, no. 260)

Dickinson was able to "enclose" her name by putting her name on a card and placing it within its own envelope inside the letter. She also enclosed the poems "Safe in their Alabaster Chambers," "The nearest Dream recedes unrealized," "We play at Paste," and "I'll tell you how the Sun rose" and asked Higginson for his impression of them.[15] In fact, "Safe in their Alabaster Chambers" is a famous example of poem history and letter history converging. In 1861 Sue offered Dickinson constructive criticism about the poem. The 1859 version reads:

> Safe in their Alabaster Chambers –
> Untouched by Morning
> And untouched by Noon –
> Sleep the meek members of the Resurrection –
> Rafter of satin,
> And Roof of stone.
>
> Light laughs the breeze
> In her Castle above them –
> Babbles the Bee in a stolid Ear,
> Pipe the Sweet Birds in ignorant cadence –
> Ah, what sagacity perished here
>
> (*P* 100, no. 216)

Sue disliked the second stanza, which introduces babbling bees and singing birds – sweet and frothy natural images that do not seem to fit with the cold, quiet funeral monuments, the "Alabaster Chambers." Dickinson responded to Sue's criticism, revising the second stanza. "Perhaps this verse would please you better," she writes, then includes (*L* 379, no. 238):

> Grand go the Years – in the Crescent – above them –
> Worlds scoop their Arcs –
> And Firmaments – row –
> Diadems – drop – and Doges – surrender –
> Soundless as dots – on a Disc of Snow –
>
> (*P* 100, no. 216)

Remarkably, the new stanza incorporates crisp, biting, complex images – "Diadems," "Doges," "dots," and a "Disc." Although the first version uses some alliteration with "Babbles," "Bee," and "Birds," the new stanza takes alliteration and runs even farther with it, piling "d's" and "s's" in the last two lines. There is also an economy of language in the second version that borrows imagery from the heavens as well as the sciences: "Crescent," "Arcs," "Firmaments,"

"Disc," and "Snow." The second version is a poetic feat, far more complex and engaging than the "babbling bee" version.

Ironically, Susan was not pleased with the new version that resulted from her comments. She preferred the original stanza after all. Dickinson, however, favored the revision. When Sue sent the poem to the *Republican* for publication, she chose the first version. When Dickinson sent the same poem to Higginson for feedback, she sent the second version.[16]

Essentially unpublished in her own lifetime, Dickinson's habit of distributing poems to her friends through her letters became her primary method of "publishing" her work. The medium of the letter not only allowed her to customize the poem for the recipient but it allowed Dickinson to preserve the personal touch that she felt was edited away in typesetting and publication. Examining the manuscripts Dickinson left behind and the text of the letters also reveals how poetic her letters are. Her commitment to powerful words does not begin or end with her poems; it is a part of her letter-writing as well. Letters often enclosed poems which were indistinguishable from the text of the letter itself. Thus, it is almost impossible to separate an examination of Dickinson's poems from her letters; they are intimately connected. Emily Dickinson's interest in every detail of existence, along with the great pains she took to make her letters artistic creations in themselves, require readers to examine both her letters and her poems.

Sweeping with many-colored brooms: the influence of the domestic

At a time when New England welcomed industrialization, Emily Dickinson celebrated the value of something far closer to home: the domestic realm. She resented the industrialization that rapidly changed the face of New England, realizing that the shifts toward urban centers, anonymous work, and profit motives would quickly eclipse values that were dear to her: family, friendship, and individualism. Through her life, poetry, and letters, Dickinson fought to preserve the role of the home against the onslaught of machinery and money. Her solution, however, was not merely to revert back to Victorian ideals of housewifery and homemaking. Instead, she fought both the Victorian ideal of the home and the industrialization ideal of the city to express her own unique vision for the future.

It is easy to assume that Emily Dickinson's devotion to her family and home was merely a product of Victorian society. Essential requirements of a woman in the 1800s were fostering and maintaining an economic and structured household and creating a loving home that acted as a sanctuary for the family. Although Dickinson did adhere to many domestic requirements of an unmarried woman, she also bent and twisted gender roles and expectations to meet her own ends, especially to develop the craft of writing. Unable to have an office or workplace of her own, Dickinson created one out of the kitchen hearth, the verdant garden, and the small writing table in her upstairs bedroom. Rather than a recluse or victim of Victorian society, Dickinson was "a pioneer who chose the domestic as her frontier because it provided the freedom to write."[17] In addition to the physical space and time to write, the domestic realm also provided themes, settings, analogies, and metaphors for her poetry and letters.

To understand the societal expectations and conflicts that shaped Dickinson's position within the house, and in turn, the house's position in her writing, it is helpful to examine the views of womanhood and domesticity in the 1800s. Edward Dickinson gave his daughters a mixed blessing by sending them to school. He believed the girls should be well educated and work on their studies, but that once they physically left school, they had to leave it mentally as well.[18] Emily and Lavinia Dickinson received an education almost identical to what their brother Austin received. However, by the time they turned eighteen, the girls were expected to leave science, literature, and philosophy behind in favor of learning to please a husband and build a home.[19] Dickinson did her duties for her family, but at times resented the work, which she humorously describes to her friend Abiah Root in this May 1850 letter:

> I have been at work, providing "the food that perisheth," scaring the timorous dust, and being obedient, and kind . . . I am yet the Queen of the court, if regalia be dust, and dirt, have three loyal subjects, whom I'd rather releive from service. Mother is still an invalid tho' a partially restored one – Father and Austin still clamor for food, and I, like a martyr am feeding them. Would'nt you love to see me in these bonds of great despair, looking around my kitchen, and praying for such deliverance . . . *My* kitchen I think I called it, God forbid that it was, or shall be my own – God keep me from what they call *households*, except that bright one of "faith"!   (*L* 99, no. 36)

Dickinson used her letters to voice objections that she may not have had the liberty to say in public. She may have been venting steam, or perhaps her letters chronicle a slowly developing plan for survival. Either way, she was beginning to challenge expectations for women that were considered irrefutable fact. Her father's stern, unrelenting views of womanhood were ideas that were celebrated in the society and literature of the time. Perhaps the most famous literary work that embodied these views is Coventry Patmore's 1863 narrative poem, *The Angel in the House*. The English poet wrote this work in honor of his fiancée, their marriage, and their devotion to one another. *The Angel in the House* celebrates a woman's meekness, virtue, childlike qualities, and unequivocal devotion to her husband. The icon of the "Angel in the House" ignited future feminist writers Charlotte Perkins Gilman and Virginia Woolf, who railed against the image in their own writing as they sought to break free of it in their lives. The Dickinsons, who shared books and exchanged letters about the books they were reading, would have been familiar with this immensely popular work. In fact, Austin Dickinson gave Sue a copy of *The Angel in the House: The Betrothal* for their second Christmas together.[20] The book obviously had a strong impact upon Sue, who eventually quoted it in Dickinson's obituary.

According to Patmore's vision, a household "angel" has "light-hearted ignorance" of masculine "discourse," the very topics that Edward Dickinson wanted his daughters to leave behind after their schooling.[21] Patmore's angel also "strives to please" because

> Man must be pleased; but him to please
> Is woman's pleasure; down the gulf
> Of his condoled necessities
> She casts her best, she flings herself.[22]

Perhaps the most objectionable assertion for Emily Dickinson is Patmore's poem "The Metamorphosis":

> Maid, choosing man, remember this:
> You take his nature with his name.
> Ask, too, what his religion is,
> For you will soon be of the same.[23]

Dickinson had a highly original, controversial, and rebellious "nature" and religion. Perhaps she already knew that to choose a man was to take his own belief system over her own and Dickinson was unwilling to surrender her beliefs.

If the spiritual and emotional height of a woman's life was to marry and devote her life to her husband, what was the role for women who did not marry? It was a question that Dickinson increasingly faced with each passing year as an unmarried woman. Despite several male admirers and friends, neither Dickinson daughter married. "The shift from their father's to their husband's homes meant that wives had to relinquish their primary bonds, and Emily Dickinson was not willing to undo these ties."[24] Dickinson's single status provided her with a viable alternative. By "remaining single in a society that placed enormous burdens on wives," Dickinson could spend all of her efforts on writing poetry.[25]

From the time they were young, Emily and Lavinia Dickinson assumed the responsibilities of cooking, cleaning, sewing, drawing fresh water, and maintaining heat and light in their family's home. When she was fifteen years old, Dickinson wrote to her friend Abiah Root about the stacks of mending waiting for her:

> I found a quantity of sewing waiting with open arms to embrace me, or rather for me to embrace it, and I could hardly give myself up to "Nature's sweet restorer," for the ghosts of out-of-order garments crying for vengeance upon my defenceless head. However, I am happy to inform you, my dear friend, that I have nearly finished my sewing for winter, and will answer all the letters which you shall deem worthy to send so naughty a girl as myself.   (*L* 40, no. 14)

In this letter, Dickinson uses her wit to express the burden of housework and her own selfish desire to escape it in order to write. She gives piles of clothes arms to hold her, mouths to scream, and apparitional bodies. Her vivid imagination takes a mere pile of a laundry and whips it into "out-of-order garments crying for vengeance." Although she self-deprecatingly calls herself "naughty" for loathing her chores, her playful tone hints at a certain pride in fighting the ghostly garments to make time for writing friends. Girls like Dickinson were expected to assume these tasks not only to maintain their family's households, but also as preparation for a future life building a household with their husbands. Like the "naughty" young woman battling the clothes in the letter, Dickinson and her sister had other ideas.

"By their socially active teenage years, Emily and her sister, Lavinia, rebelled against the ongoing demands of labor-intensive work necessary to maintain their prominent family," writes Aife Murray, a scholar who has studied the connections between the Dickinson family and their servants.[26] Victorian New England was changing from a rural, agrarian society where domestic labor was done exclusively by the women of the family to an urban, industrial society where wealthier families could afford domestic help. The Dickinson family employed local black and itinerant white workers as well as long-term Irish servants.[27] There was a large labor pool of Irish immigrants in New England, since the Irish potato famine in the 1840s had sent many Irish abroad. Servants helped provide a measure of freedom from the burdens of running a household. Murray notes that Dickinson's sharp increase in the number of poems she wrote correlates with the time the family hired its first permanent maid, an Irishwoman named Margaret O'Brien.[28]

The first Dickinson servants, including Margaret O'Brien, were later followed by long-term Irish servants such as Margaret Maher and her brother-in-law, Thomas Kelley, in 1869. Domestic servants gave Dickinson the freedom to pursue her writing. The servants who worked within the Dickinson home were also extensions of the family. In fact, both the servants and family members spent a great deal of time in the kitchen. It was a place for writing letters, reading books, and catching up on daily activities as well as cooking and eating meals.[29] Because many of Dickinson's later manuscripts were written on scraps of paper from the kitchen, including bills, recipes, and food wrappers, it is likely that she found inspiration there and quickly wrote on any paper she could find.[30] She was also acutely aware of her surroundings and may have gone to the kitchen expressly to write about it.

The influence of the kitchen, hearth, and fire can be seen in many of Dickinson's poems. Literal uses of the kitchen and hearth occur in poems where Dickinson describes physical or emotional warmth, such as "ruddy fires on the hearth –" (*P* 54, no. 115). She also uses the hearth metaphorically to describe the light of God or love in one's soul. For example, in poem 638, she writes, "To my small Hearth His fire came – / And all my House aglow" (*P* 316, no. 638).

If the kitchen and domestic realm were prominent themes within Dickinson's poetry, an important subset of this topic is the image of baking. On 25 September 1845, the fourteen-year-old Dickinson wrote:

> I am going to learn to make bread to-morrow. So you may imagine
> me with my sleeves rolled up, mixing flour, milk, salaratus, etc., with a
> deal of grace. I advise you if you don't know how to make the staff
> of life to learn with dispatch. I think I could keep house very
> comfortably if I knew how to cook. But as long as I don't, my knowledge
> of housekeeping is about of as much use as faith without works, which
> you know we are told is dead. Excuse my quoting from the Scripture,
> dear Abiah, for it was so handy in this case I couldn't get along very
> well without it.   (*L* 20, no. 8)

In the letter, Dickinson provides specific details of rolled sleeves, mixing flour, and saleratus (sodium bicarbonate for leavening) to help her friend picture the scene. In contrast to the list of ingredients, however, she also aligns the work of baking with religion: the baker has "grace" and makes "the staff of life," but because she cannot cook, Dickinson has "faith" without the action to support it. For Dickinson, there was nothing sacrilegious in aligning a baker's recipe for bread with the Scripture's recipe for salvation.

She mastered the art of baking bread and when it was time to divide chores with Lavinia, that was the task she chose. Bread had a special relevance to Dickinson, who won a prize in 1856 for her rye and Indian bread. Edward Dickinson refused to eat any loaves but those that his elder daughter baked, a fact that gave Dickinson great pride.

Bread also provided Dickinson with a wealth of metaphors. The word "bread" has many resonances that Dickinson utilizes to the fullest. At any point in her poems, "bread" can indicate hunger, poverty, or sustenance. More importantly, the word can relate to physical, emotional, or spiritual nourishment, especially when related to the "bread of life," or Eucharist consumed during communion. Dickinson frequently aligns the humble food baked in the kitchen with the promise of heavenly salvation, such as "consecrated bread" (*P* 61, no. 130), "Bread of Heaven" (*P* 570, no. 1314), and "Bread is that Diviner thing / Disclosed to be denied" (*P* 545, no. 1240). These are just a few examples of how Dickinson was able to see the transcendent in the quotidian. In Dickinson's hands, mere yeast and flour become "mystic Bread" (*P* 488, no. 1077).

When describing minutiae, the humble, seemingly inconsequential everyday details that in fact encapsulate larger truths, Dickinson often uses the image of breadcrumbs. Tiny morsels, broken off from loaves, can in fact create a trail leading back to God. They can also represent the smallest request for food or friendship:

> "Hope" is the thing with feathers –
> That perches in the soul –
> And sings the tune without the words –
> And never stops – at all –
>
> And sweetest – in the Gale – is heard –
> And sore must be the storm –
> That could abash the little Bird
> That kept so many warm –
>
> I've heard it in the chillest land –
> And on the strangest Sea –
> Yet, never, in Extremity,
> It asked a crumb – of Me.
>
> (*P* 116, no. 254)

Because she imagines "Hope" as a soft songbird, a "thing with feathers," Dickinson shows that even the smallest portion of oneself, a single "crumb," can provide an entire meal for Hope. According to the poem, Hope is personal ("perches in the soul"), tireless ("And never stops – at all"), resilient ("in the chillest land"), fearless ("on the strangest Sea"), and heroically strong ("never, in Extremity, / It asked a crumb"). Dickinson embodies the self-sacrifice and towering strength of Hope as a surprisingly fragile, insignificant vessel: a song-bird. The Hope-bird never asks for breadcrumbs, but it is implied that the speaker provides them out of love for the creature/feeling. The poem demonstrates that the tiniest amount of one's soul, the smallest amount, freely given, can keep Hope alive.

Large-scale forms such as political speeches, jeremiads, and epics were successful and celebrated male models of expression in the nineteenth century, but Dickinson understood that images from daily life, including mere domestic chores, were just as valid and expressive of woman's experience. She took everyday domestic tasks of baking bread, sewing samplers, quilting, and sweeping and elevated them to the spiritual level. In her poems, a common woman cleaning her kitchen becomes Aurora sweeping the sky:

> She sweeps with many-colored Brooms –
> And leaves the Shreds behind –
> Oh Housewife in the Evening West –
> Come back, and dust the Pond!
>
> You dropped a Purple Ravelling in –
> You dropped an Amber thread –
> And now you've littered all the East
> With Duds of Emerald!
>
> And still, she plies her spotted Brooms,
> And still the Aprons fly,
> Till Brooms fade softly into stars –
> And then I come away –
>
> (*P* 101, no. 219)

As the housewife sweeps, the poem travels through the progression of a sunset: the sun sinking into the West, purple streaks of light, the yellow sun dropping below the horizon, the green earth, and finally the night sky. Dickinson gives her housewife authority over the heavens, making her an active participant through striking, active verbs. The housewife's near-mythic power, combined with the closeness of "Brooms," "fly," and "into stars" may also suggest another powerful female image, particularly for a woman writing in Massachusetts: the witch. Regardless of whether or not Dickinson intended that association, it is important to note that she presents a powerful woman who transcends mere housework and "leaves the Shreds behind" while ambitiously heading unfettered, straight for the skies.

Thomas Wentworth Higginson notes that Dickinson's home was "a house where each member runs his or her own selves" (*L* 473, no. 342a). Dickinson took the idea of the home as private haven and pushed it one step further, allowing the home to take the place of church and even heaven itself. In 1862, when her town was caught up in the frenzy of a religious revival, Dickinson writes a poem in which she radically refuses to leave her home to attend church:

> Some keep the Sabbath going to Church –
> I keep it, staying at Home –
> With a Bobolink for a Chorister –
> And an Orchard, for a Dome –
>
> (*P* 153, no. 324)

In this poem (the complete poem is on p. 92), Dickinson provides natural substitutions for the religious fixtures inside a church. For Dickinson, there is no contradiction between avoiding church and honoring God, for "Home is the definition of God" (*L* 483, no. 355). In her modest bedroom, Dickinson erected a cathedral to friendship and love. Dickinson embraced the home as her occupation, base, and inspiration, staying exclusively within The Homestead and celebrating the domestic in her writing. Therefore, it is fitting that when Austin had to fill in his sister's occupation on her death certificate, he wrote, "At Home."

Blasphemous devotion: biblical allusion in the poems and letters

Emily Dickinson's overt use of biblical language and metaphor has often caused her to be classified as a "religious" or even a "Christian" poet. While there can be no doubt that religious language and even specific biblical quotations are an important part of her work, Dickinson's use of the Bible is unorthodox. Indeed, many of her references to the Bible can easily be interpreted, according to strictly evangelical notions of piety, as impious and possibly even blasphemous. As in other aspects of her writing, Dickinson's project is often one of reversal, even in her use of Scripture. She uses biblical allusion to reverse the expected object of religious devotion from God to earth/nature/friend, to reverse the relationship of creature and creator, and thus to reverse the existing hierarchy of authority. This is not to say that Dickinson had no "faith," but that whatever "faith" she might have had she often chose to express in non-traditional terms. While scholars can argue incessantly about whether or not Emily Dickinson was a "Christian," it is obvious from the poems and letters themselves that Dickinson does not use the Bible in a traditionally devotional way.

Not only does Dickinson tend to undermine the traditional authority of the Bible by referencing it playfully and ironically, she uses these references to exalt what would normally be considered earthly (and thus secondary) relationships to a religious level. "The Bible is an antique Volume," written about 1882 according to Johnson's dating, is an important example of Dickinson's tendency to toy impiously with biblical authority:

> The Bible is an antique Volume –
> Written by faded Men
> At the suggestion of Holy Spectres –
> Subjects – Bethlehem –
> Eden – the ancient Homestead –
> Satan – the Brigadier –
> Judas – the Great Defaulter –
> David – the Troubadour –
> Sin – a distinguished Precipice
> Others must resist –
> Boys that "believe" are very lonesome –
> Other Boys are "lost" –
> Had but the Tale a warbling Teller –
> All the Boys would come –
> Orpheus' Sermon captivated –
> It did not condemn –
>
> (*P* 644, no. 1545)

This poem mockingly describes the Holy Spirit's inspiration of Scripture as the "suggestion of Holy Spectres," speaks of Eden as "the ancient Homestead," calls Satan a "Brigadier" and David "the Troubadour" (instead of the Psalmist), and refers to the saved and lost as "Boys." In this poem, the language of Scripture lacks the force of the pagan Orpheus story because it judges instead of captivating its audience with a beautiful story of love, as Orpheus did. Relegating the theology of judgment to the province of "faded Men" and "Boys," to a male-centered view of the universe, Dickinson's own worldview embraces a more feminine perspective of earth and community.

Although such outspoken and aggressive skepticism is common in Dickinson's later poems, subtler indications of doubt are also apparent in much earlier poems. In the poem "If the foolish, call them '*flowers*' –" (1860), for example, Dickinson hints at her skepticism by using quotation marks that suggest the fictiveness of the biblical stories to set off references to "Revelations," "Moses," "Canaan," and God's "Right hand" (*P* 79, no. 168). "You're right – 'the way *is* narrow' –," written just a year later (1861), also employs quotation marks to signal the doubt Dickinson feels about biblical doctrines, but the poem is much more obviously skeptical and critical of biblical authority.

You're right – "the way *is* narrow" –
And "difficult the Gate" –
And "few there be" – Correct again –
That "enter in – thereat" –

'*Tis* Costly – So are *purples*!
'Tis just the price of *Breath* –
With but the "Discount" of the *Grave* –
Termed by the *Brokers* – "*Death*"!

And after *that* – there's Heaven –
The *Good* Man's – "*Dividend*" –
And *Bad* Men – "go to Jail" –
I guess –   (*P* 107, no. 234)

Dickinson undercuts the biblical pronouncement of Matthew 7:14 ("[S]trait is the gate, and narrow is the way, which leadeth unto life, and few there be that find it") not only by using quotation marks but also by employing the masculine language of business and commerce in her contemplation of salvation. Salvation is a questionable transaction between God and men who earn salvation's dividends or are sent to jail for their faulty investments. Dickinson punctuates words like "Discount," "Dividend," and "Jail" in exactly the same way as she does Christ's pronouncement on salvation – with dashes and quotation marks – thus equating biblical "truth" and questionable business rewards. As if this blasphemous equation were not enough, Dickinson undermines the biblical quotation further with the poem's abrupt final line, "I guess." Dickinson is expressing not just doubt but a mocking disbelief.

Dickinson's skepticism can be traced back to 1850 when many of her friends and family were part of a religious revival in Amherst. The pressures Dickinson felt "to accept Christ as her Savior" at Mount Holyoke were intense, and Dickinson felt torn between her fear of alienation from both God and her friends and a commitment to her own personal convictions and experience. Her vacillation is evident in a letter to her friend Abiah Root:

> Abiah, you may be surprised to hear me speak as I do, knowing that I express no interest in the all-important subject, but I am not happy, and I regret that last term, when that golden opportunity was mine, that I did not *give up* and become a Christian. It is not now too late, so my friends tell me, so my offended conscience whispers, *but it is hard for me to give up the world*.   (*L* 67, no. 23, emphasis mine)

For the young Dickinson, to "become a Christian" is to "give up" a part of herself, the part that treasures "the world." As she told her friend Abiah earlier, "I know not why, I feel that the world holds a predominant place in my affections.

I do not feel that I could give up all for Christ, were I called to die" (*L* 38, no. 13). Unable to experience God's presence in the powerful way that others claimed to and that was expected of her, Dickinson began timidly to question God's presence. In a letter to Abiah Root in 1850, Dickinson explains her struggles to believe:

> What shall we do my darling, when trial grows more, and more, when the dim, lone light expires, and it's dark, so very dark, and we wander, and know not where, and cannot get out of the forest – whose is the hand to help us, and to lead, and forever guide us, they talk of a "Jesus of Nazareth," will you tell me if it be he?   (*L* 98, no. 36)

Unable to feel that "God, and Heaven are near," to hear his "'still small voice'" and to consider "the life she has always led . . . black, and distant" the way that her friend Abby Wood does after her religious conversion experience (*L* 98, no. 36), Dickinson seems to grow more skeptical about this "Jesus of Nazareth." Unable to relate to her friends' religious experiences, Dickinson aligns herself in this letter with the "bad ones" and with "Satan" himself (*L* 98, no. 36). Unsure that "there's such a person / As 'a Father' – in the sky" (*P* 99, no. 215), Dickinson registers her alienation in one poem as a banishment:

> I'm banished – now . . .
> How foreign that can be –
> You'll know – Sir – when the Savior's face
> Turns so – away from you –
> (*P* 117, no. 256)

The distance that Dickinson felt separated her from a personal God continued to grow. Her poem "I meant to have but modest needs –" registers this divide from a personal God, especially in its last two stanzas:

> I left the Place, with all my might –
> I threw my Prayer away –
> The Quiet Ages picked it up –
> And Judgment – twinkled – too –
> That one so honest – be extant –
> It take the Tale for true –
> That "Whatsoever Ye shall ask –
> Itself be given You" –
>
> But I, grown shrewder – scan the Skies
> With a suspicious Air –
> As Children – swindled for the first –
> All Swindlers – be – infer – .
> (*P* 229–30, no. 476)

For Dickinson, to pray is merely to "throw" her words "away," to waste the power of language on an unresponsive "Swindler" who has told her a fictitious "Tale" of answered prayer. God is definitely distant if he exists at all. In her description of her family to T. W. Higginson in 1862, Dickinson's feelings about their God are expressed with poignant clarity: "They are religious – except me – and address an Eclipse, every morning – whom they call their 'Father'" (*L* 404, no. 261). By 1882, Dickinson registers an even more aggressive skepticism: God's "Right Hand" is not merely marked as fictional by quotation marks; "That Hand is amputated now / And God cannot be found" (*P* 646, no. 1551). The right hand that should be extended to his children on earth is cut off; there is no possibility of intimacy with a personal God.

Dickinson's priorities were clear early in her life and poetic career. As early as 1853, Dickinson's dedication to this life, this world, and her earthly friends became apparent. Her use of Scripture was a tactic she employed to express not her devotion to a personal God but to her friends, as this letter to her close friends the Hollands makes apparent:

> If prayers had any answers to them, you were all here to-night, but I seek and I don't find, and knock and it is not opened. Wonder if God is just – presume he is, however, and t'was only a blunder of Matthew's.
> I think mine is the case, where when they ask an egg, they get a scorpion, for I keep wishing for you, keep shutting up my eyes and looking toward the sky, asking with all my might for you, and yet you do not come.   (*L* 263–4, no. 133)

The playful way in which she undercuts the authority of Matthew's gospel by accusing the apostle of a "blunder" could easily be considered impious. But her letter becomes almost blatantly blasphemous when we consider the implications of her prayer. A fundamentalist might argue that the reason Dickinson does not get her "wish" – notice that she talks about "wishing" not praying – is that her request is not theologically sound. Dickinson references Matthew 7:7–11, which promises that the Father will give "good gifts" to those who ask him, but the parallel passage in Luke 11, which Dickinson must have known, sheds more light on the inappropriate nature of her request.

> Ask, and it shall be given you; seek, and ye shall find; knock, and it shall be opened unto you. For every one that asketh receiveth; and he that seeketh findeth; and to him that knocketh it shall be opened. If a son shall ask bread of any of you that is a father, will he give him a stone? or if he ask a fish, will he for a fish give him a serpent? Or if he shall ask an

egg, will he offer him a scorpion? If ye then, being evil, know how to give good gifts unto your children: how much more shall your heavenly Father *give the Holy Spirit to them that ask him*?

(Luke 11:9–13, emphasis mine)[31]

Dickinson has replaced the appropriate "prayer" for the presence of the Holy Spirit with a "wish" for the presence of her friends the Hollands. Emily Dickinson simultaneously undermines traditional ideas of biblical authority (in this case the gospels of Matthew and Luke) and exalts something else (in this case her friends) to God's place. Dickinson reverses the position of creature and creator, reducing God's authoritative Word to a "blunder" and placing her friends in the position of the Holy Spirit. Friends not only form the community of saints for Emily Dickinson, they quite often replace, at least rhetorically, God or Christ himself. Her priorities are clear once again in an 1856 letter to Elizabeth Holland: "Pardon my sanity . . . in a world *in*sane, and love me if you will, for I had rather *be* loved than to be called a king in earth, or a lord in Heaven" (*L* 329–30, no. 185).

In a letter to Abiah Root written on 19 August 1851, Emily Dickinson uses the words Christ spoke the night before his crucifixion during the Last Supper (John 14:3, 16:16) to heighten the importance of her separation from Abiah: "'Yet a little while I am with you, and again a little while and I am *not* with you' because you go to your mother" (*L* 129, no. 50). Abiah's separation from Dickinson is thus equated with Christ's separation from his disciples after his ascension and before his second coming. Similarly, Dickinson draws on biblical images of God and Christ as a protecting rock to describe her friendship with Susan Gilbert.[32] Susie, not Christ, is Dickinson's "sweet shelter [and] covert from the storm" (*L* 181, no. 77).[33] As with Abiah, Dickinson uses Christ's words to signal the importance of Susie's absence: "you [Susie]," she laments, "I have 'not always'" (*L* 175, no. 73). The biblical story that Dickinson quotes here comes from Matthew 26. As a woman anoints Jesus' head as an act of worship and as a symbol of his coming death and burial, the disciples complain that the costly ointment should have been sold and the money given to the poor. Jesus, however, rebukes them: "Why trouble ye the woman? for she hath wrought a good work upon me. For ye have the poor always with you; but *me ye have not always*" (Matthew 26:10–11, emphasis mine). In Dickinson's letter, Susie replaces Christ as the object worthy of worship and self-denial; it is for Susie, not Christ, that Dickinson must "deny [herself] and take up [her] cross" (*L* 176, no. 73, cf. Matthew 16:24). Dickinson conjures Susie's presence, not Christ's, when she references Christ's promise to his disciples that "where two or three are gathered together in my name, there am I in the midst of them" (Matthew

18:20): "'[T]wo or three' are gathered in your name, [Susie,] loving you, and speaking of you – and will you be there in the midst of them?" (*L* 183, no. 77). As Susie rhetorically replaces God, her letters take on extreme importance as well; they become the heavenly treasures that "moth" and "rust" cannot corrupt (*L* 183, no. 77; cf. Matthew 6:19–20). Dickinson's purpose in quoting these Biblical passages is not to encourage a reverence toward God or to establish his authority. Rather, she uses the biblical language to reverse the hierarchy of worship:

> So sweet and still, and Thee, Oh Susie, what need I more, to make my heaven whole?
>
> . . .
>
> I have thought of [seeing you again] all day, Susie, and I fear of but little else, and when I was gone to meeting it filled my mind so full, I could not find a *chink* to put the worthy pastor; when he said "Our Heavenly Father," I said "Oh Darling Sue"; when he read the 100th Psalm, I kept saying your precious letter all over to myself, and Susie, when they sang . . . I made up words and kept singing how I loved you, and you had gone, while all the rest of the choir were singing Hallelujahs.
>
> (*L* 201, no. 88)

Worship is owed not to God but to friends, especially to her female friends. To Frances Norcross, she says, "[W]hat shall I render unto Fanny, for all her benefits?" (*L* 367, no. 225), again using Fanny as a replacement for the Psalmist's God: "What shall I render unto the Lord for all his benefits toward me?" (Psalm 116:12). Dickinson is not concerned with the promise of Christ's love ("[N]either death, nor life, nor angels, nor principalities, nor powers, nor things present, nor things to come, Nor height, nor depth, nor any other creature, shall be able to separate us from the love of God, which is in Christ Jesus our Lord" (Romans 8:38–9)); she is concerned with the love she shares with her female friends: "Susie . . . for what shall separate us from any whom we love – not '*hight* nor depth'" (*L* 145, no. 56).

In contrast, Dickinson uses the Bible in a letter to Austin to undercut his authority and position as a son and heir: "[Y]ou resign so cheerfully your birthright of purple grapes . . . that I hardly can [enjoy them] . . . They are so *beautiful* Austin – we have such an *abundance* 'while *you* perish with hunger'" (*L* 137, no. 53). Here Dickinson alludes to the story of Jacob and Esau, in which Esau sells his birthright to Jacob for a bowl of pottage because he is supposedly "perish[ing] with hunger" (Genesis 25:29–34). She seems to suggest that despite his birthright as the only son, Austin has relinquished a more precious natural birthright, a link to the earth that Emily has maintained, in order to enter the world of business. Emily, though seemingly sympathizing with Austin's inability to enjoy his "birthright of grapes," is also undermining his birthright as a son and claiming her own possession of a more important birthright – nature itself.

Dickinson's transfer of devotion from God to friends is a part of her poetry as well as her letters. "He forgot – and I – remembered" (*P* 95, no. 203), for example, suggests that relations between friends carry as much significance as the relationship between Christ and his disciples.

> He forgot – and I – remembered –
> 'Twas an everyday affair –
> Long ago as Christ and Peter –
> "Warmed them" at the "Temple fire."
>
> "Thou wert with him" – quoth "the Damsel"?
> "*No*" – said Peter, 'twasn't me –
> Jesus merely "looked" at Peter –
> Could I do aught else – to Thee?

Forgetting a friend is as serious an offence to Dickinson as Peter's denial of Christ (Luke 22:54–62). Friendship is raised to the level of a religious experience, a faith that should never be denied or discarded. Thus, when her uncle Joel Norcross fails to write her as he promised, Dickinson sends a long, scathing, though playful letter that prophetically judges his silence (*L* 77–81, no. 29). Likewise in 1883, she writes to Maria Whitney,

> Dear Friend,
>   You are like God. We pray to Him, and He answers "No." Then we pray to Him to rescind the "no," and He don't answer at all, yet "Seek and ye shall find" is the boon of faith.
>   You failed to keep you appointment with the apple-blossoms . . .
>
> (L 780, no. 830)

Dickinson registers the failure of a friend to keep a promise or an appointment so strongly that she likens it to God's failure to answer prayer.

Dickinson's faith and devotion then are not directed to God. She has already doubted and perhaps denied him. Instead, friends become one of the centers of her faith and love. Her poem "I cannot live with You –" (*P* 317–18, no. 640) provides yet another example of her insistence on placing earthly relationships above God. In this poem, the narrator contemplates her own and her lover's deaths, imagining that she cannot rise to an afterlife because "Your Face / Would put out Jesus." The narrator tells her lover she "could not" serve heaven "Because You saturated Sight – / And I had no more Eyes / For sordid excellence /

As Paradise." Paradise is but a "sordid excellence" compared with the human relationship she has with this person. Again, Dickinson's interest in this life and its relationships usurps the power and excellence of the spiritual and heavenly realms.

Perhaps even more important than her view of friendship as a religious experience is Dickinson's interest in and exaltation of the natural world to a religious and transcendent level. Heaven and God become secondary to the natural world and its tiny creatures, and love of nature becomes faith. Earthly life, rather than salvation, becomes the important prize. Instead of salvation being the "pearl of great price" for which one gives up everything else (Matthew 13:46), "life" is that "Enormous Pearl" (*P* 213, no. 444). Life in its minutest details and briefest experiences is what interests Dickinson as the greatest of treasures. So, for example, when in an early letter to Abiah Root, Dickinson references the passage in Matthew 6:20 that admonishes believers to "lay up for yourselves treasures in heaven, where neither moth nor rust doth corrupt," she confesses that her own inclination is to look "*earthward*" toward the "treasure *here*" on earth (*L* 130, no. 50). This inclination causes Dickinson to become instantly distracted from the words of Scripture by the image of the moth:

> this makes me think how I *found* a little moth in my stores the other day – a very *subtle* moth that had in ways and manners to me and mine unknown, contrived to hide itself in a favorite worsted basket – how long my little treasurehouse had furnished an arena for it's destroying labors it is not *mine* to tell – it had an *errand* there – I trust it fulfilled it's mission; it taught me dear Abiah to have no treasure *here*, or rather it tried to tell me in it's little mothy way of another *enduring* treasure . . . How many a lesson learned from lips of such tiny teachers
>
> (*L* 130, no. 50)

The moth becomes Dickinson's teacher, but the instruction that it "trie[s] to tell [her]" is less important to Dickinson than the moth itself, which is "found" like a treasure and is capable of being "subtle" and having a "mission." Dickinson does not quite learn the lesson to lay up treasures in heaven because she is too fascinated with the treasures this world offers: the moth, her friendship with Abiah, and the contents of her worsted basket. As one of her letters to Susan suggests, Dickinson's concern lies in the things of the earth: "You know how I must write you, down, down, in the terrestrial" (*L* 181, no. 77). Dickinson chose the world, despite others' warnings of her soul's danger: "But the world allured me & . . . I listened to her syren voice . . . Friends reasoned with me & told me of the danger I was in . . . but I had rambled too far to return & ever since my heart has been growing harder & more distant" (*L* 30–1, no. 11).

This earth-centered allure constantly drives Dickinson to contemplate God's promised interest in detail: "Are not two sparrows sold for a farthing? and one of them shall not fall on the ground without your Father" (Matthew 10:29).[34] Several of Dickinson's poems specifically reference this passage (nos. 141, 164, 237, 690, etc.), and they all suggest that Dickinson doubts God's concern for nature's details. As a result, she chooses to usurp God's place and become herself the faithful and devoted observer and recorder of nature's details, details like the moth she describes in her letter to Abiah. No flower's petal or bee's wing goes unnoticed by Dickinson.

Since her project then is to invest the things of this world with religious and devotional significance, Dickinson employs biblical language to describe and worship the details of the natural world. Thus, the mouse of poem 61 is worthy of God's kingdom and of receiving his own "mansion" where he can "nibble" all day in "seraphic Cupboards" (*P* 32, no. 61). This poem blasphemously parodies Jesus' promise to his disciples – "In my Father's house are many mansions" (John 14:2) – and ascribes an importance to the mouse that most would consider disproportionate to its tiny place in nature. The physical world is for Dickinson inherently spiritual, and thus the mouse deserves the same place in heaven that a human soul might receive. For the same reason, the material body is not subordinate to the spirit in Dickinson's mind. She scoffs at the idea that the body is "sown in corruption" and "dishonor" (I Corinthians 15:42–3):

> "Sown in dishonor"!
> Ah! Indeed!
> May *this* "dishonor" be?
> If I were half so fine myself
> I'd notice nobody!
>
> "Sown in corruption"!
> Not so fast!
> Apostle is askew!
> Corinthians I. 15. narrates
> A Circumstance or two!
>   (*P* 32, no. 62)

Nature is powerful and transcendent for Dickinson and deserves veneration and worship. "I can't tell you – but you feel it" (*P* 34, no. 65) establishes the importance and necessity of showing a reverence for nature by referencing Isaiah 6, a vision of the throne room of God where the seraphim cover their faces, presumably to avoid seeing God's overwhelming glory. This allusion in the third stanza not only pokes fun at the biblical account but also suggests that nature, an "April Day," should receive similar worship:

> I can't tell you – but you feel it –
> Nor can you tell me –
> Saints, with ravished slate and pencil
> Solve our April Day!
>
> Sweeter than a vanished frolic
> From a vanished green!
> Swifter than the hoofs of Horsemen
> Round a Ledge of dream!
>
> Modest, let us walk among it
> With our faces veiled –
> As they say polite Archangels
> Do in meeting God!
>
> Not for me – to prate about it!
> Not for you – to say
> To some fashionable Lady
> "Charming April Day"!
>
> Rather – Heaven's "Peter Parley"!
> By which Children slow
> To sublimer Recitation
> Are prepared to go!   (*P* 34, no. 65)

To call this experience of nature merely a "Charming April Day" is blasphemy akin to taking God's name in vain (stanza 4). For Dickinson, summer is a "Sacrament" and "Last Communion" (*P* 61, no. 130). She "never believed [Paradise] to be a superhuman site" (*L* 508, no. 391); indeed, the glories of this earth make "[God's] Paradise superfluous" (*L* 329, no. 185) because in Dickinson's mind this supposedly "corruptible" earth (I Corinthians 15:42) "has already [put on Incorruption]" (*L* 508, no. 391). "Earth is Heaven – / Whether Heaven is Heaven or not" (*P* 602, no. 1408). The earth is Dickinson's paradise, her heaven, her Eden (*P* nos. 239, 413, 575, 1069, 1657), and the tiny creatures of earth are her gods. "'Heaven' is . . . The Apple on the Tree – ," the "Color, on the Cruising Cloud – " (*P* 109, no. 239). With such an interest in this world, it is not surprising that Dickinson prays not in the name of the Father, the Son, and the Holy Spirit, but "In the name of the Bee – / And of the Butterfly – / And of the Breeze – Amen!" (*P* 14, no. 18). For Dickinson, nature is her revelation, "The Revelations of the Book / Whose Genesis was June" (*P* 502, no. 1115). When trying to imagine how "Heaven" could be more glorious than the earth, Dickinson's imagination fails. She sees the earth's revelations as her senses experience them, instead of imagining potential glories beyond them:

> "Heaven" has different Signs – to me –
> Sometimes, I think that Noon
> Is but a symbol of the Place –
> And when again, at Dawn,
>
> A mighty look runs round the World
> And settles in the Hills –
> An Awe if it should be like that
> Upon the Ignorance steals –
>
> The Orchard, when the Sun is on –
> The Triumph of the Birds
> When they together Victory make –
> Some Carnivals of Clouds –
>
> The Rapture of a finished Day –
> Returning to the West –
> All these – remind us of the place
> That Men call "Paradise" –
>
> Itself be fairer – we suppose –
> But how Ourself, shall be
> Adorned, for a Superior Grace –
> Not yet, our eyes can see –
>
> (*P* 280–1, no. 575)

Here again "Heaven" and "Paradise" are enclosed in quotation marks, marking them as suppositional, possibly fictional. Though seemingly attempting to see the earth's beauties as "Signs" and "symbol[s]" of "the place / That Men call 'Paradise,'" Dickinson's focus is actually on those beauties of the earth that her senses can detect. Her qualifiers that she only "sometimes" thinks of noon as "a symbol of the Place," and that her ignorance wonders "if it [heaven] should be like that [dawn]" point to her interest not in paradise but in the earth she sees. The earth's revelations are so powerful that they encompass Dickinson's attention, making her wonder if "the place that men call 'Paradise'" could be like these earthly wonders. Paradise is a place that men "suppose" is "fairer" than the earth, but Dickinson cannot see how earth can be surpassed. Her eyes cannot see how it "shall be / Adorned, for a Superior Grace" because she already sees nature as revelatory. Her language draws on common metaphors for Christ. Instead of viewing noon and dawn as signs and symbols of a coming paradise that, upon his return, Christ will establish in a new heaven and earth, they are revelatory in themselves. She speaks not of the coming triumph and victory of a returned Messiah who will reign over a perfect kingdom, but of the "Triumph of the Birds / When they together Victory make." Dickinson speaks not of the rapture of the saints at Christ's return but of the "Rapture of a finished Day – / Returning to the West." The day becomes the salvific figure of renewal in itself instead of a sign for Christ and the renewal that he, Christians suppose, will bring. Enraptured by what her senses can detect in this life, Dickinson is unable to imagine anything more beautiful or revelatory, as is evident in an 1870 letter: "O Matchless Earth –," she writes, "We underrate the chance to dwell in Thee" (*L* 478, no. 347). For Dickinson, "Nature is Heaven" (*P* 332, no. 668). Nature is her Bible, her Genesis to Revelation, and thus she uses biblical language to establish the natural world as worthy of attention and devotion.

Dickinson was not interested in being a religious or devotional poet in the traditional sense. She *was* devotional; but her devotion, though expressed in biblical language, was often transferred to this world – to her friends and to nature. Inverting the normal arc of devotional poetry, Dickinson directed her thoughts *downward* to the earth and the present life, discovering in it things worthy of true attention and adoration. For Dickinson, the Bible merely provided the vocabulary with which she could express her own devotion to the treasures this world has to offer.

"Easy, quite, to love": friendship and love in Dickinson's life and works

Forever questioning and finally abandoning any hope of an intimate and potentially eternal relationship with a personal God, it is not surprising that Emily Dickinson invested her attention in earthly, human relationships. For Dickinson, heaven is to be "found below" and the people who inhabit this heavenly earth become as important to her as "Angels" or saints (*P* 644, no. 1544), as important as God is to those with deep religious faith. For Dickinson, calling her friends and lovers "Angels" was much more than a sentimental term of endearment, but a deeply felt and genuinely expressed sense of their importance. Of course, such a highly charged investment in her relationships was a double-edged sword. Just as Dickinson's commitment to experiencing the present to its fullest brought Dickinson moments not only of transcendent ecstasy but also of deepest despair verging on chaos and breakdown, her deep commitment to her relationships brought not only joyful and transcendent communion but deep

anguish, betrayal, and abandonment. These painful moments would sometimes spark hurt, melancholy responses from Dickinson or strong rebukes and
assurances of her independence. Dickinson's own struggle for autonomy often
clashed with her deep desire for real, meaningful communion with others.
These contradictory desires especially influenced her relationships with men.
Desiring to be considered an equal, but also longing to be accepted, Dickinson
at times asserted herself above the judgments and opinions of her male friends,
while at other times she almost groveled for acceptance. What seems true of
all of Dickinson's relationships is that they were stormy and complicated for
the very reason that they were deeply important to her. As with all her experiences, the smallest moment carried the greatest significance and thus carried
the potential for ecstasy or desolation.

The deep and meaningful companionship that Emily Dickinson derived
from her female friends was an intense and important part of her emotional
life. Always very close to her sister Lavinia, Dickinson also had long and
deep friendships with her sister-in-law Susan Dickinson (to whom she wrote
more than 150 extant letters) and with Elizabeth Holland. Dickinson also kept
up a hearty and loving correspondence with her cousins Louise and Frances
Norcross until her death, despite their being twelve and fifteen years younger
than Dickinson. She often addressed all of these women as her dear "sisters."
Her early friendships with Jane Humphrey and Abiah Root were very important
to her as well, although she lost touch with them after they married and moved
away from Amherst. Indeed, Dickinson felt a deep, personal connection to
her female friends; for her, they formed a community that shared confidences,
anxieties, deep emotions, and comforting consolations.

Because she formed extremely strong attachments to those with whom she
was close, Dickinson used religious and romantic language to express her love
for her friends in both her poems and letters. Such expressions of love are often
evident in Dickinson's letters to Susan Gilbert Dickinson, even before Susan
became her sister-in-law, as seen in this letter to Sue in 1852:

> Will you let me come dear Susie – looking just as I do, my dress soiled
> and worn, my grand old apron, and my hair – Oh Susie, time would fail
> me to enumerate my appearance, yet I love you just as dearly as if I was
> e'er so fine . . .
> The dishes may wait dear Susie – and the uncleared table stand, *them* I
> have always with me, but you, I have "not always" – *why* Susie, Christ
> hath saints *manie* – and I have *few*, but thee – the angels shant have
> Susie – no – no no! . . .
> . . .

> Oh my darling one, how long you wander from me, how weary I grow of waiting and looking, and calling for you; sometimes I shut my eyes, and shut my heart towards you, and try hard to forget you because you grieve me so, but you'll never go away . . . say, Susie, promise me again, and I will smile faintly – and take up my little cross again of sad – *sad* separation.   (*L* 175–6, no. 73)

This letter is a wonderful example of the religious and romantic rhetoric that Dickinson used over and over again in her letters to Susan and to her other close friends. The twenty-one-year-old Dickinson finds comfort and communion not in the presence of Christ, but Sue. Indeed, she inverts the usual hope of religious devotion and casts herself in the role of a disciple who must deny herself to follow not Christ, in this case, but Sue. By loving Susan so deeply, Dickinson is actually violating the biblical passage that she quotes from: "He that loveth father or mother more than me [Christ] is not worthy of me: and he that loveth son or daughter more than me is not worthy of me. And he that taketh not his cross, and followeth after me, is not worthy of me" (Matthew 10:37–8). Sue, not Christ, is the object of this self-denying love. Of course the tone of the letter is exaggerated, but the separation from Susie seems to Dickinson a painful eternity. In another letter of 1852, Dickinson writes:

> Susie, will you indeed come home next Saturday, and be my own again, and kiss me as you used to? . . . I hope for you so much, and feel so eager for you, feel that I *cannot* wait, feel that *now* I must have you – that the expectation once more to see your face again, makes me feel hot and feverish, and my heart beats so fast – . . .
> . . .
>   Why, Susie, it seems to me as if my absent Lover was coming home so soon.   (*L* 215–16, no. 96)[35]

Dickinson's deep connection to her friends generates expectations for a reciprocal response from them, which is not always forthcoming. This leads Dickinson to feel betrayed or abandoned.

Dickinson's friends often found themselves receiving rebukes in the form of ironic metaphors for their failures to respond to her letters, to reciprocate unceasingly her avowals of deep love and devotion. When Susan, for example, fails to write back promptly enough, Dickinson writes that she is "fond even tho' forsaken" and that she tries "not to think unkind thoughts, or cherish unkind doubt concerning" Susan (*L* 222, no. 103). So in the same letter that Abiah Root hears from Dickinson that "I love to sit here alone, writing a letter to you," she is also rebuked for her failure to respond:

Very likely, Abiah, you fancy me at home in my own little chamber, writing you a letter, but you are greatly mistaken. I am on the blue Susquehanna paddling down to you; I am not much of a sailor, so I get along rather slowly . . . Hardhearted girl! I don't believe you care, if you did you would come quickly and help me out of this sea; but if I drown, Abiah, and go down to dwell in the seaweed forever and forever, I will not forget your name, nor all the wrong you did me!

Why did you go away and not come to see me? I felt so sure you would come, because you promised me, that I watched and waited for you, and bestowed a tear or two upon my absentee. How very sad it is to have a confiding nature, one's hopes and feelings are quite at the mercy of all who come along; and how very desirable to be a stolid individual, whose hopes and aspirations are safe in one's waistcoat pocket, and *that* a pocket indeed, and one not to be picked!

Notwithstanding your faithlessness I should have come to see you, but for that furious snow-storm; I did attempt in spite of it, but it conquered in spite of me.   (*L* 166–7, no. 69)

Dickinson likens her letter to a romantic journey in which she is in danger of drowning because her lover will not come to her rescue. But the letter is only half playful. Abiah is chided for failing to visit, despite the terrible snow-storm. Dickinson's "confiding nature" is injured by her friend's "faithlessness."

The intensity of Dickinson's affection often strained her relationships with her friends. Abiah Root and Jane Humphrey gradually dropped off from Dickinson's correspondence, and even her friendship with Susan seemed at times to suffer. Dickinson had such deep feelings and her love was so intense that any quarrel took on magnified proportions. It was difficult for Dickinson's friends to live up to the expectations of her love, to respond adequately enough to her sometimes obsessive love for them. Susan frequently received passionate letters expressing Dickinson's powerful love:

Oh Susie, I would nestle close to your warm heart, and never hear the wind blow, or the storm beat, again. Is there any room there for me, or shall I wander away all homeless and alone? Thank you for loving me, darling, and *will* you "love me more if ever you come home"? – it is enough, dear Susie, I know I shall be satisfied. But what can I do toward you? – *dearer* you *cannot* be, for I love you so already, that it almost breaks my heart – perhaps I can love you *anew*, every day of my life, every morning and evening – Oh if you will let me, how happy I shall be!

. . . Never mind the letter, Susie; you have so much to do; just write me every week *one line*, and let it be, "Emily, I love you," and I will be satisfied.   (*L* 177, no. 74)

The intensity of such feelings places a great demand on its recipient to reciprocate with similar expressions of devotion.

Dickinson's love was often mingled with doubt of an equal response, as she registers in an early poem:

> You love me – you are sure –
> I shall not fear mistake –
> I shall not *cheated* wake –
> Some grinning morn –
> To find the Sunrise left –
> And Orchards – unbereft –
> And Dollie – gone!
>
> I need not start – you're sure –
> That night will never be –
> When frightened – home to Thee I run –
> To find the windows dark –
> And no more Dollie – mark –
> Quite none?
>
> Be sure you're sure – you know –
> I'll bear it better now –
> If you'll just tell me so –
> Than when – a little dull Balm grown –
> Over this pain of mine –
> You sting – again!   (*P* 73–4, no. 156)

This poem illustrates Dickinson's desire to be "sure" of her friends' love. The repetition of the words "you are sure" shows a near-obsession with securing the other's love and a painful doubt whether that love will remain strong. In this poem, the failure to love fully is "to cheat" the author, to abandon her completely. Again, the obsessive emphasis on reliability underscores the repeated motif of abandonment, first at sunrise and then at nightfall. The pain of such abandonment is unbearable, but it is not unfamiliar; and Dickinson makes it clear she does not want to be vulnerable to Susie's emotional vagaries: "I'll bear it better now . . . than . . . when you sting again."

With such high expectations for her friendships, it is not surprising that when Dickinson did quarrel with her friends, those quarrels were as intense as her expressions of love. Having argued with Susan, evidently about religious matters, Dickinson writes a letter whose language could not be stronger:

> Sue – you can go or stay – There is but one alternative – We differ often lately, and this must be the last.
>
>   You need not fear to leave me lest I should be alone, for I often part with things I fancy I have loved, – sometimes to the grave, and sometimes

to an oblivion rather bitterer than death – thus my heart bleeds so
frequently that I shant mind the hemorrhage, and I only add an agony to
several previous ones, and at the end of day remark – a bubble burst!
. . .

Few have been given me, and if I love them so, that for *idolatry*, they
are removed from me – I simply murmur *gone*, and the billow dies away
into the boundless blue, and no one knows but me, that one went down
today. We have walked very pleasantly – Perhaps this is the point at
which our paths diverge – then pass on singing Sue, and up the distant
hill I journey on.   (*L* 305–6, no. 173)

These painful antagonisms or misunderstandings destabilize Dickinson's emotional life, even though in this letter she defensively claims that she is strong
enough to withstand such damage. In spite of Dickinson's pronouncement, she
and her sister-in-law remained friends until Emily Dickinson's death. Dickinson would once again describe herself as "Susan's Idolator" who "keeps a Shrine
for Susan" (*L* 458, no. 325). More than twenty years later, Dickinson's love for
Susan is still apparent, as is evident in a short poem written in 1877:

To own a Susan of my own
Is of itself a Bliss –
Whatever Realm, I forfeit, Lord,
Continue me in this!
        (*P* 600, no. 1401)

Communion in this life through companionship with Susan gives Dickinson
ecstatic "Bliss" for which she is willing to "forfeit" other "Realm[s]," perhaps
even a place in God's kingdom.

As her letters to Susan and to Abiah Root make clear (*L* 166–7, no. 69),
Dickinson's intense love for her friends sometimes undermines her desire for
independence, an independence already hampered and complicated by societal
expectations such as the imperative expectation to experience a religious conversion, which Dickinson refused in order to preserve herself. Perhaps the most
threatening to Dickinson's desire for independence were "the cultural edicts
against female autonomy."[36] In an era that demanded that children submit to
their fathers, Dickinson struggled with her own father over her poetic pursuit.
Her letter to Higginson describing her family suggests her father's ambivalence
regarding her intelligence: "[My father] buys me many Books – but begs me
not to read them – because he fears they joggle the Mind" (*L* 404, no. 261).
Though she remained at home, Dickinson won the fight with her father for
autonomy; he eventually gave her the largest bedroom in the house – with the
best view – and allowed her to relinquish many household duties in order to
sleep late and write poetry into the night. Dickinson longed to carve out her

own destiny, not to accept conventional arrangements, as she confided often to Susan:

> It is such an evening Susie, as you and I would walk and have such pleasant musings, if you were only here – perhaps we would have a "Reverie" after the form of "Ik Marvel," indeed I do not know why it would'nt be just as charming as of that lonely Bachelor, smoking his cigar – and it would be far more profitable as "Marvel" *only* marveled, and you and I would *try* to make a little destiny to have for our own.
>
> (*L* 144, no. 56)

Dickinson's desire to be free to experience adventures like those only imagined by the bachelor hero of Ik Marvel's (Donald Mitchell's) *Reveries of a Bachelor* is complicated by gender. As a woman, she is not free to imagine bachelor adventures for herself, let alone to enact them. Indeed, women were not expected to have a destiny of their own but to share the destiny of a husband. Dickinson's view of marriage and sexuality, however, indicates a fear of losing oneself to the will of another.

In 1852, she writes a powerful lament for the lost lives of women to marriages that eclipse their selfhood:

> How dull our lives must seem to the bride, and the plighted maiden, whose days are fed with gold, and who gathers pearls every evening; but to the *wife*, Susie, sometimes the *wife forgotten*, our lives perhaps seem dearer than all others in the world; you have seen flowers at morning, *satisfied* with the dew, and those same sweet flowers at noon with their heads bowed in anguish before the mighty sun; think you these thirsty blossoms will *now* need naught but – *dew*? No, they will cry for sunlight, and pine for the burning noon, tho' it scorches them, scathes them; they have got through with peace – they know that the man of noon, is *mightier* than the morning and their life is henceforth to him. Oh, Susie, it is dangerous, and it is all too dear, these simple trusting spirits, and the spirits mightier, which we cannot resist! It does so rend me, Susie, the thought of it when it comes, that I tremble lest at sometime I, too, am yielded up.   (*L* 210, no. 93)

While Dickinson understands the delights of love and sexuality, the price of marriage seems much too costly. Wives are expected to suffer and submit to the scorching "man of noon," the husband who is to be their head and to whom they forfeit their lives. For Dickinson, the price of marriage is the sacrifice of one's will, the "yielding up" of one's self, a price too high to pay. Dickinson's desire for independence and autonomy is threatened by traditional expectations for women – marriage and dutiful submission.

These stifling social norms affected Dickinson's relationships with men throughout her lifetime. While desiring independence, Dickinson also longed for close friendship and acceptance. Her relationship with her father was thus a stormy one, and while Dickinson was bold enough to make certain demands of him, their arguments often left her feeling shut out when she desired to be accepted by him. Her relationship with her brother was likewise complicated by the differences between them. Obviously treasured by their father as his only son and heir,[37] Austin received many advantages that Dickinson herself desired. While Emily Dickinson's formal education was shortened by her father's command that she return and remain at home, Austin was able to complete a much fuller education, finishing college and receiving a degree from Harvard Law School. Dickinson longed for opportunities to see the world, to be independent, and to experience the life that Austin enjoyed. As a result, despite her deep love for her brother, Dickinson at times felt compelled to assert herself as her brother's equal or even his superior. She even constructed her own confinement to the domestic space as an advantage over Austin's required labor in the world because it allowed her to observe nature in its exquisite detail and gave her time to write her poetry. Dickinson cleverly transformed the constraint of domesticity into an advantage, eventually choosing to isolate herself almost completely from the world as an act of self-assertion and autonomy.

In order to be the poet of the family, Emily Dickinson had to be extremely assertive because Austin also wrote poems on occasion:

> And Austin is a Poet, Austin writes a psalm. Out of the way, Pegasus, Olympus enough "to him," and just say to those "nine muses" that we have done with them!
>
> Raised a living muse ourselves, worth the whole nine of them. Up, off, tramp!
>
> Now Brother Pegasus, I'll tell you what it is – I've been in the habit *myself* of writing some few things, and it rather appears to me that you're getting away my patent, so you'd better be somewhat careful, or I'll call the police!   (*L* 235, no. 110)

Declaring Austin's own poetry inferior, Emily Dickinson claims the role of poet and warns him off, accusing him of encroaching on her territory. "Rejecting passive inspiration, she announces to Austin that as a woman she had direct access to her creative energy and does not need external assistance [from the nine muses]: she herself has 'raised a living muse.' Relegating Austin to the instrumental role of Pegasus, the winged horse ridden by the Muses, Emily Dickinson assumes a proprietary stance insisting that she will protect her interest in any way necessary."[38]

The need to assert and defend her territorial position conflicts with Dickinson's desire to be loved and accepted. When she feels belittled in her relationships, especially with men, she paradoxically strikes a pose of haughty regality while also shrinking herself into an unoffending smallness. When Dickinson wrote to Higginson to ask for his advice on her poetry, his comments were not encouraging. That Dickinson wrote to him in the first place suggests her desire to publish, but when he wrote to her that he did not recommend any such attempts, Dickinson's response projects disinterest, even disdain, at the same time that it suggests a desire for Higginson's acceptance:

> I smile when you suggest that I delay "to publish" – that being foreign to my thought, as Firmament to Fin –
> If fame belonged to me, I could not escape her – if she did not, the longest day would pass me on the chase – and the approbation of my Dog, would forsake me – then – My Barefoot-Rank is better –
> You think my gait "spasmodic" – I am in danger – Sir –
> You think me "uncontrolled" – I have no Tribunal.
> Would you have time to be the "friend" you should think I need? I have a little shape – it would not crowd your Desk – nor make much Racket as the Mouse, that dents your Galleries –
> . . .
> But, will you be my Preceptor, Mr. Higginson?   (*L* 408–9, no. 265)

Posing as indifferent to Higginson's discouragement by claiming never to have desired publication, Dickinson coyly refutes Higginson's criticisms, choosing the approbation of her dog before the acceptance of the world. She mocks his opinion of her poetic innovations with a reference to her "spasmodic gait" and suggests that no tribunal judges her. But, in this same letter, Dickinson asks that Higginson accept her as a friend and become her "Preceptor," claiming that her inoffensive smallness and insignificance will scarcely inconvenience him by crowding his desk or making too much noise. The image of smallness, however, is a pose designed to make her seem inoffensive while she mocks and dismisses his criticisms. The desire to be considered equal, to assert herself, and the opposite desire to be accepted, cause Dickinson to adopt opposing roles, especially in her friendships and romantic relationships with men: at times she represents herself as a queen; at others, a tiny, unoffending mouse or bird.

Dickinson's puzzling "Master" letters are the most obvious examples of her struggles with a passionate love that threatens to dominate her and usurp her will. These three letters, probably written between 1858 and 1862,[39] have been the subject of scholarly debate for decades. Since the letters are addressed only to "Master" and are only draft copies found among Emily Dickinson's papers after her death, it is impossible to know whether they were ever sent to anyone, much less to whom they were written. There are numerous theories about the identity of "Master"; Samuel Bowles, Charles Wadsworth, T. W. Higginson, and God have all been named as the recipients of these letters. More recently, Ruth Owen Jones has suggested that William Smith Clark, an Amherst neighbor and former classmate of Austin who taught botany, zoology, and chemistry at Amherst College, was likely the "Master" whom Dickinson addressed.[40] Some have even suggested that Dickinson's reference to "Master" may in fact refer to her creative self.[41] While theories about who "Master" might have been indulge readers' gossipy interest, ultimately they are only speculations. What can be known is that these letters record Dickinson's intense passion for someone who ultimately does not return her deep love; they record her desire to be accepted, even dominated by the man she loves. The letters are full of self-debasement; the language of smallness permeates them, though at times Dickinson also seems to be expressing a sense of her real worth. For Dickinson, "[t]he romantic self is not only filled with desire and passionate yearning, but is even willing to capitulate to a master, to accept its weakness and dependence on another's strength and will . . . [T]he creative self wants to survive and prevail as an autonomous being."[42] The "Master" letters employ the romantic trope of the beloved as a god to be worshipped by the self-abased slave or sinner. The letters are "written from the point of view of a little girl who is pleading for acceptance,"[43] though there are glimpses of the strong autonomous self that Dickinson would ultimately become.

The first "Master" letter, written "about 1858" according to Johnson's dating (*L* 333, no. 187), is not as self-debasing as the other "Master" letters; it is more hopeful and expresses Dickinson's deep love for her "Master" in "sensuous language"[44]:

> Dear Master
>   I am ill, but grieving more that you are ill, I make my stronger hand work long eno' to tell you. I thought perhaps you were in Heaven, and when you spoke again, it seemed quite sweet, and wonderful, and surprised me so – I wish that you were well.
>   I would that all I love, should be weak no more. The Violets are by my side, the Robin very near, and "Spring" – they say, Who is she – going by the door –
>   Indeed it is God's house – and these are gates of Heaven, and to and fro, the angels go, with their sweet postillions – I wish that I were great, like Mr. Michael Angelo, and could paint for you. You ask me what my flowers said – then they were disobedient – I gave them messages. They

said what the lips in the West, say, when the sun goes down, and so says the Dawn.
. . .
    Each Sabbath on the Sea, makes me count the Sabbaths, till we meet on shore . . . I cannot talk any more tonight, for this pain denies me.
    How strong when weak to recollect, and easy, quite, to love.

(*L* 333, no. 187)[45]

Dickinson's love here is so strong that she is more concerned about her "Master's" illness than her own and compels herself to proclaim her love to him despite the pain it causes her. Her letter is filled with the sensuous images of "Spring" that promise renewal and that she draws on to comfort her ailing "Master." Though Dickinson does not obviously abase herself, the tone of her letter suggests weakness and smallness; she is not "great, like Mr. Michael Angelo." The respectful "Mr." she places before his name seems to suggest her own inferiority but also playfully mocks the disparity between the painter's greatness and her modest position. Though she wishes to paint at her Master's request and for his pleasure, Dickinson professes her inability to capture the scene; yet, at the same time, she proceeds to paint a verbal portrait of spring. Her submission also seems undercut by the disobedience of her flowers, which playfully refuse to answer her Master, though they whisper that he is her sun, as is evident from the other letters in this series in which Dickinson calls herself "Daisy." "Emily Dickinson uses the traditional metaphor of the daisy or 'day's eye' that follows the sun's path across the sky to describe the romantic relationship between a dependent woman and a powerful man."[46] The image hearkens back to Dickinson's fear that women become dominated by their submissive love for their husbands; they "cry for sunlight, and pine for the burning noon, tho it scorches them, scathes them" (*L* 210, no. 93). The love that Dickinson expresses in these letters threatens to undermine her will.

    The second "Master" letter, written about 1861 according to Johnson, confirms that the "Master" does not return "Daisy's" love. The letter employs the language of wounding that is so prominent in Dickinson's complaints against friends, but she does not adopt the powerful, disdainful pose she assumes so often in response to disappointments in friendship and love. Confused by her powerful feelings, Dickinson conveys a childlike fragility and vulnerability:

> Master.
>   If you saw a bullet hit a Bird – and he told you he was'nt shot – you might weep at his courtesy, but you would certainly doubt his word.
>   One drop more from the gash that stains your Daisy's bosom – then would you *believe*? . . . God made me – Master – I did'nt be – myself. I

don't know how it was done. He built the heart in me – Bye and bye
it outgrew me – and like the little mother – with the big child – I got
tired holding him . . . I am older – tonight, Master – but the love is the
same . . . If it had been God's will that I might breathe where you
breathed – and find the place – myself – at night – if I never forget that
I am not with you . . . if I wish with a might that I cannot repress –
that mine were the Queen's place – the love of the Plantagenet is my
only apology –   (*L* 373–4, no. 233)

Dickinson at first registers herself as a small, frail, and wounded "Bird" and then
as a weak "little mother" unable to carry the child that is her heart because of its
weighty burden of love. Yet, she also declares her "wish" to have "the Queen's
place" at her Master's side, claiming that her love is "the love of the Plantagenet"
and thus worthy of royal place.

However, despite her desire to occupy a commanding position, Dickinson
continues to insist on her comparative smallness: "Daisy's arm is small – and
you have felt the horizon hav'nt you" (*L* 374, no. 233). Though Dickinson
recognizes that her Master's power over her threatens to kill her autonomous
self ("I used to think when I died – I could see you – so I died as fast as
I could" (*L* 374, no. 233)), she seems unable to shake his control; though
she realizes that she has fallen into a dependent, self-consuming love for a
powerful man who does not show mercy or concern, Dickinson is consumed
by her passion and unable to alter her love: "I don't know what you can
do for it – thank you – Master – but if I had the Beard on my cheek – like
you – and you – had Daisy's petals – and you cared so for me – what would
become of you? Could you forget me in fight, or flight – or the foreign land?"
(*L* 374, no. 233). Dickinson is trapped by this love which borders on obsession.
Her position as a dependent woman in nineteenth-century America does not
allow her the escapes available to men: "fight, or flight – or the foreign land."
"Passion" has its origins in the word "suffer," but Dickinson later transmutes her
vulnerability and emotional suffering into an advantage that allows her to write
poems mapping the soul's terrain by exploring intensely the emotions of each
moment.

Dickinson's final letter to the "Master" is, once again, full of humiliating self-
abasement which is a cry for acceptance. The depth of her passion frightens
her, yet she is compelled to beg Master to accept her love; it is a "love so big it
scares her [Daisy], rushing among her small heart – pushing aside the blood
and leaving her faint and white in the gust's arm –" (*L* 391, no. 248). Using
the language of self-diminution, Dickinson attempts to convince her Master to
forgive whatever fault in her has displeased him:

> Oh, did I offend it – Daisy – Daisy – offend it – who bends her smaller life
> to his meeker every day – who only asks – a task – something to do for
> love of it – some little way she cannot guess to make that master glad –
> . . .
>
>   Daisy – . . . who would have sheltered him in her childish bosom –
> only it was'nt big eno' for a Guest so large – *this* Daisy – grieve her
> Lord – and yet it often blundered – Perhaps she grieved his taste –
> perhaps her odd – Backwoodsman ways teased his finer nature. Daisy
> knows all that – but must she go unpardoned – teach her, preceptor
> grace – teach her majesty – Slow at patrician things – Even the wren
> upon her nest learns more than Daisy dares –   (*L* 391, no. 248)

Dickinson diminishes herself not only by highlighting her smallness and
fragility, but also by calling herself backward, "slow" and dull and begging her
Master to grant her grace and "teach her majesty." Using conventions of Romantic literature which portrays the beloved as a god, Daisy begs to be forgiven:

> Low at the knee . . . Daisy kneels a culprit – tell her her fault – Master – if
> it is small eno' to cancel with her life, she is satisfied – but punish dont
> banish her – shut her in prison, Sir – only pledge that you will forgive –
> sometime – before the grave, and Daisy will not mind – She will awake
> in your likeness.   (*L* 391, no. 248)

Daisy grovels for forgiveness, offering to be punished if necessary. Highlighting
her Master's exalted position, Dickinson/Daisy references David's Psalm: "I
will behold thy face in righteousness: I shall be satisfied, when I awake, with thy
likeness" (Psalm 17:15). Desiring to be cleansed and forgiven of her faults by
her Master, Dickinson not only claims that she will be satisfied with her Master
alone, but also that she is willing to be remade in his likeness, to be shaped
according to his desire. Daisy will be whatever Master wants; accepting her
and her love will not inconvenience his greatness because her own smallness
will not disturb him:

> Master – open your life wide, and take me in forever, I will never be
> tired – I will never be noisy when you want to be still. I will be your best
> little girl – nobody else will see me, but you – but that is enough – I shall
> not want any more – and all that Heaven only will disappoint me – will
> be because it's not so dear   (*L* 392, no. 248)

Because her Master's denial of her "stabs her more" than any physical pain she
feels, Dickinson is willing to submerge herself, to become quiet and unoffending
– a good girl – just as she promised Higginson in an earlier letter (*L* 408–9, no.
265). But here Dickinson takes her self-diminution to the utmost extreme. She

is not only willing to be small and quiet but completely invisible and unavailable to anyone else. She is willing to be absorbed into her Master's desires.

While the emotions expressed in the "Master" letters are painfully self-defeating and border on self-annihilation, Dickinson survived the painful experience they record:

> While exploring her impulse for self-abnegation and renunciation, she permitted herself to shrink almost to nothingness. But she held on and did not extinguish herself. She is numbed by her fear, but she survives and actually emerges stronger from the conflict. In doing so, she successfully resists the Romantic tradition that casts women in subordinate roles – her sense of self survives and even triumphs over an extraordinarily powerful cultural paradigm that threatens to destroy her. Dickinson's "Master" poems and letters are efforts to resolve her conflicts with a rejecting man. Struggling with her feelings of grief and rage, she is finally able to accept these emotions. Eventually she is able to reclaim the energy and power that she had assigned to the significant men in her life, whether God, her father, Bowles, or Higginson.[47]

Two poems, written according to Johnson's dating during the period of the "Master" letters, demonstrate the re-emergence of Dickinson's autonomous and creative self from the struggle of the "Master" letters: "Title divine – is mine!" and "I'm ceded – I've stopped being Theirs –" both express Dickinson's "increasing autonomy."[48]

"Title divine – is mine!" takes an ironic look at the marriage state, registering it as both a "shrouding," or burial, and a birth into sexuality. In this poem Dickinson seems to reject the possibility of marriage because it stifles, or "shrouds" the self that she believes is royal:

> Title divine – is mine!
> The Wife – without the Sign!
> Acute Degree – conferred on me –
> Empress of Calvary!
> Royal – all but the Crown!
> Betrothed – without the Swoon
> God sends us Women –
> When you – hold – Garnet to Garnet –
> Gold – to – Gold –
> Born – Bridalled – Shrouded –
> In a Day –
> Tri Victory
> "My Husband" – women say –
> Stroking the Melody –
> Is *this* – the way?   (*P* 487, no. 1072)

In this difficult and complex poem, Dickinson claims a regality for herself despite lacking the royal ornaments that are the signs of a wife. She is an "Empress," though an "Empress of Calvary" – of suffering.[49] Her suffering, however, has resulted in victory and has made her an empress, as Christ was made a king by claiming victory over death in his resurrection. Dickinson is "Royal" despite not bearing the "Sign" of matrimony or experiencing the erotic/orgasmic "Swoon" of the wedding night. The wedding kiss between lips of "Garnet," and the wedding rings of "Gold" bind permanently, but the chiming "Garnet to Garnet – / Gold – to – Gold" echoes not the marriage service but the funeral service: "Earth to earth, ashes to ashes, dust to dust." The bride is not merely "Born" into a new life of sexuality but also "Bridalled" (a play on bride and bridled), both made a bride and bridled like a horse to be controlled by her husband; she is also "Shrouded" – her autonomous self is now dead – buried beneath her husband's wishes and surname. Dickinson seems happy to escape from such a marriage, even though her freedom is predicated on "Acute" suffering.

In "I'm ceded – I've stopped being Theirs –" Dickinson claims control over her life, putting aside the name and position given her by society and choosing her own destiny:

> I'm ceded – I've stopped being Theirs –
> The name They dropped upon my face –
> With water, in the country church
> Is finished using, now,
> And They can put it with my Dolls,
> My childhood, and the string of spools,
> I've finished threading – too –
>
> Baptized, before, without the choice,
> But this time, consciously, of Grace –
> Unto supremest name –
> Called to my Full – The Crescent dropped –
> Existence's whole Arc, filled up,
> With one small Diadem.
>
> My second Rank – too small the first –
> Crowned – Crowing – on my Father's breast –
> A half unconscious Queen –
> But this time – Adequate – Erect,
> With Will to choose, or to reject,
> And I choose, just a Crown –

> (*P* 247, no. 508)

In this poem, Dickinson has stopped belonging to her society, to her father who "dropped" her name on her at her christening/baptism. Such an existence was for her "childhood" and is to be left behind with her "Dolls." Her first existence was *given* to her, but her "second Rank" is one that Dickinson claims for herself; she chooses an existence and a destiny of her own. She has been "Called to my Full," called to a vocation and an existence that includes a "Diadem." She is no longer the "half unconscious Queen" whose first rank given her by her father when she was a baby "Crowing" on his chest was "too small." She now is "Adequate" unto herself and willfully chooses a "second Rank" for herself that is "just a Crown." She is not baptized by another but baptizes herself unto a new calling, a poetic vocation. "In addition to being the sign of royalty, 'Crown' refers to the ancient laurel wreath awarded to poets; 'ceded' refers to Dickinson herself – she is the territory that others must relinquish; self-centered, she now claims the right to devote her energy to her own work."[50] Dickinson no longer belongs to others; she is her own "Master," and she will relinquish her self to no one.

As we have seen, Dickinson's deep desire for love and friendship often led her to a dependence on others that conflicted with her desire for independence. While Dickinson continued to cherish her friendships, she never allowed those relationships to threaten her autonomy completely as she did in her tumultuous and torturous relationship with Master. She continued to revel in the pleasures and joy of friendships and to feel the despair of loss and betrayal and channeled these powerful emotions into her poetry, recording the intense feelings of the moment without losing her creative, autonomous self. Love and friendship were of such primary importance to Dickinson that they could both elate and wound her. Dickinson was able to overcome pain by recording these contradictory moments; she learned to triumph over such wounds through acceptance. Dickinson never abandoned the value of love despite the heartache it brought and continued to cherish her small community of women that supported one another, and to send letters full of love and advice to friend and family alike. She also continued her friendships with Higginson, Bowles, and other men, listening to their advice regarding her poetry, though choosing herself whether or not to follow it.

Likewise, Dickinson did not reject romantic love but carried on a passionate correspondence with Judge Otis Lord from 1858 to 1883, a correspondence which lacks the kind of painful self-abasement present in her "Master" letters. In contrast, she writes about Judge Lord: "I confess that I love him – I rejoice that I love him – I thank the maker of Heaven and Earth – that gave him me to love – the exultation floods me" (*L* 614–15, no. 559). While Dickinson's passion for Lord is obvious ("The withdrawal of the Fuel of Rapture does not withdraw the Rapture itself. Like Powder in a Drawer, we pass it with a Prayer, it's Thunders only dormant" (*L* 786, no. 842)), her letters to him are playful, especially in comparison to her humiliating letters to "Master"; she places herself on a much more equal footing with the judge, to whom she considered marriage: "Emily 'Jumbo'! Sweetest name, but I know a sweeter – Emily Jumbo Lord. Have I your approval?" (*L* 747, no. 780). Dickinson's friendships and loves continued to be of utmost importance to her, but they no longer destabilized her sense of self as they did in her youth; she came to accept love's heartache and disappointment as part of the contradictions of life and love. Her friends were of such importance to her that Dickinson counted them as her "few" saints, and each loss of a friend was a devastating loss: "Forgive the Tears that fell for few," she wrote to Elizabeth Holland after Judge Lord's death, "but that few too many, for was not each a World?" (*L* 816, no. 890). Each of Dickinson's friends was a "World" of utmost importance in itself and in its relationship to her.

"The Heaven – below":[51] nature poems

Emily Dickinson's commitment to life, to this world with its complex range of emotions and relationships, also included a commitment to the physical earth. Dedicated to living a life experienced to its fullest, Dickinson celebrated the marvelous beauties of nature. But unlike the Romantics who cherished nature in its sublime magnitude, its overwhelming grandeur, Dickinson's appreciation for nature includes an appreciation for its details, its minute and often overlooked inhabitants, and its tiny pleasures. Of course, Dickinson also felt nature's sublimity and recorded it in her poetry, but more often she felt reverence for its subtle processes and intricate details. Thus, much of Dickinson's interest in nature is centered in the small spaces of her garden where she tended her treasured flowers, watched the birds and bees flit between blooms, and enjoyed the changing light and shades of daytime. She saw nature as an end in itself and not merely as a vehicle to philosophical truths. Of course, her observation of nature led her to contemplate the rhythms and meanings of life and to find correspondences between life in her garden and in human society, but unlike many Transcendentalists who saw God in and through nature, Dickinson saw nature as godlike, as worthy in itself of worship, attention, devotion. Thus, her nature poems do not always look for the meaning behind nature; she does not seek in nature a revelation of God as the Puritans and even the Transcendentalists might have. Nature is its own revelation and worthy of contemplation in and of itself.

Emily Dickinson's reverence for life led her to revere the world in which life unfolded. Dickinson dedicated herself to recording the process of life as she was able to observe it. Unfettered by economic necessity, she was able to commit herself to observing the beauty her rural community offered, and to tend the flowers in her garden, to contemplate the light and shade of the waning day. Dickinson was able to avoid the pressures of working and producing an income and to enjoy a leisurely existence supported by her father's wealth. In addition to household servants, she also had a gardener who helped her tend her plants. Dickinson appreciated the leisure that her father's wealth provided and felt at times the vulnerability of his wealth and her lifestyle: "I dreamed a dream & Lo!!! Father had failed & mother said that 'our rye field which she & I planted, was mortgaged to Seth Nims'" (*L* 48, no. 16). Though aware that industrialization would soon bring the world of commerce to Amherst (her father had a major role in bringing the railroad to Amherst), Dickinson cherished her bucolic life and "her seclusion permitted her to develop an extraordinarily vivid awareness of the natural world."[52] Her leisure gave her the opportunity to observe the details of nature in a way that "could not be sustained in a law office where her brother and father worked, or a library where her cousin Frances Norcross spent her days, or especially at the tea parties that occupied Susan Gilbert's afternoons."[53] Such deep attention to nature's plentitude led Dickinson to feel that "Earth is Heaven – / Whether Heaven is Heaven or not" (*P* 602, no. 1408) – her love for nature can only be described as worship.

Throughout her poetry, Dickinson's interest in nature's bounty is apparent. Her letters also reveal her simple love for nature: "The Frogs sing sweet – today – They have such pretty – lazy – times –" (*L* 406, no. 262). Dickinson's dashes echo the intermittent croaking of the frogs, whose lazy melody gives her intense pleasure. Rejecting the Puritan work ethic's driven and compulsive busy-ness, Dickinson embraced the slower rhythms of nature and rural life that allowed her to enjoy the world's sensory and synaesthetic richness: "The lawn is full of south and the odors tangle, and I hear today for the first the river in the tree" (*L* 452, no. 318). The following poem portrays the gentleness of the earth's rhythms by describing nature as a nurturing mother:

> Nature – the Gentlest Mother is,
> Impatient of no Child –
> The feeblest – or the waywardest –
> Her Admonition mild –
>
> In Forest – and the Hill –
> By Traveller – be heard –
> Restraining Rampant Squirrel –
> Or too impetuous Bird –

How fair Her Conversation –
A Summer Afternoon –
Her Household – Her Assembly –
And when the Sun go down –

Her Voice among the Aisles
Incite the timid prayer
Of the minutest Cricket –
The most unworthy Flower –

When all the Children sleep –
She turns as long away
As will suffice to light Her lamps –
Then bending from the Sky –

With infinite Affection –
And infiniter Care –
Her Golden finger on Her lip –
Wills Silence – Everywhere –

(*P* 385–6, no. 790)

Unlike the Puritanical God, whom Dickinson viewed as a distant and judg-mental father, nature is for Dickinson "the Gentlest Mother," both patient and nurturing. Embracing a feminine vision of the earth, Dickinson imagines Nature as a kind, careful, and graceful mother who watches over even her tiniest creatures as part of her "Household." Nature does not punish severely like a father but admonishes mildly like a caring mother. The "Rampant Squirrel" and "too impetuous Bird" are not beneath her notice and care. Indeed, nature's gentleness, her "fair . . . Conversation," and the soft music of her "Voice" trans-form her "Household" into an "Assembly" of worship where even the "minutest Cricket" and "most unworthy Flower" can offer up prayers that she will hear. Dickinson is carefully replacing God with nature, contrasting nature's gentle-ness and care with the absent figure of the Puritanical God who is supposed to watch over and care for this earth but fails to do so. Nature steals God's worship because she is more gentle, her admonitions are softer, and her care more universal. Her voice does not sound in thundering judgment and law (cf. Exodus 20) but speaks gentle and "fair . . . Conversation"; her ears are not closed to her children's "timid prayer," as Dickinson felt God's were; and her will is enforced with "infinite Affection" and "infiniter Care" like a mother who gently hushes her children to sleep, not with a father's chastising hand. Nature's rhythms are life-affirming, and thus she receives the worship and prayers of an adoring creation and of this adoring poet.

Dickinson captures her rapturous love of nature in sensuous language and images. To describe the beauty and power of nature is for Dickinson both an impossible task and the calling that she has chosen for herself.

How the old Mountains drip with Sunset
How the Hemlocks burn –
How the Dun Brake is draped in Cinder
By the Wizard Sun –

How the old Steeples hand the Scarlet
Till the Ball is full –
Have I the lip of the Flamingo
That I dare to tell?

Then, how the Fire ebbs like Billows –
Touching all the Grass
With a departing – Sapphire – feature –
As a Duchess passed –

How a small Dusk crawls on the Village
Till the Houses blot
And the odd Flambeau, no men carry
Glimmer on the Street –

How it is Night – in Nest and Kennel –
And where was the Wood –
Just a Dome of Abyss is Bowing
Into Solitude –

These are the Visions flitted Guido –
Titian – never told –
Domenichino dropped his pencil –
Paralyzed, with Gold –

(*P* 135–6, no. 291)

While this poem ends with the impossibility of artistically capturing the "Vision" of the setting sun and finished day, the rest of the poem is committed to capturing that moment with vivid language. Not only does Dickinson personify the different figures that play a part in the bewitching sunset but she uses rich, luxurious language that paints a picture and thus makes the sunset palpable. The "Mountains *drip*" with the sunset which also "*drape*[s]" the brake. The rich, sensuous sounds of "drip" and "drape" give the lines an exotic feel and cause the reader not only to see the fiery "burning" sunset but also to feel the way it seems to shimmer across the landscape like golden paint. Indeed, the moment is so full of wonderful images that the sun is called a "Wizard," whose wonderful display bewitches onlookers. The sunset is a grand ball, where steeples escort grand ladies into the assembly room and the departing sun leaves glints on the grass like those reflected from the sapphires of a duchess departing after the dance. The moment is regal and rich; "Scarlet" and precious jewels and grand ladies dazzle the scene. Dusk crawls out as the ball finishes and the stars "Glimmer" on the sky's streets like torches ("Flambeau") that "no men carry." Night encloses the world with its cathedral "Dome of Abyss" and with a gentlemanlike bow encloses the wood in solitude. The repeated "How's" of the poem function not only as exclamatory superlatives but also ask a real question that the poem tries to answer: "How can I describe the glory of such a sunset?" The regal, sensuous imagery captures the transcendent "Vision" that is the sunset, a vision that paralyzes artistic attempts to depict it in its rich "Gold[en]" beauty and power. The language throughout is rich and palpable; the images are specific and concrete. Thus, Dickinson captures the "Wizard" power of the sunset by using images not of the sunset but of a royal ball. By using an entirely different set of images, Dickinson is able to convey the beauty of the sunset and the overwhelming power it impresses on its viewers.

The image of nature as a wizard is one that Dickinson often uses to convey this world's unexplainable power over her emotions. The power of sunrise and sunset are invoked in an earlier poem that shows how even the tiniest of nature's details can enthrall Dickinson; the quiet "Murmur of a Bee" holds as much sway over Dickinson's feelings as does a beautiful sunset.

> The Murmur of a Bee
> A Witchcraft – yieldeth me –
> If any ask why –
> 'Twere easier to die –
> Than tell –
>
> The Red upon the Hill
> Taketh away my will –
> If anybody sneer –
> Take care – for God is here –
> That's all.
>
> The Breaking of the Day
> Addeth to my Degree –
> If any ask me how –
> Artist – who drew me so –
> Must tell!   (*P* 73, no. 155)

Like "Witchcraft," the sunrise and sunset, even the tiny "Murmur of a Bee" has a mysterious, inexplicable power to mesmerize Dickinson, who is utterly awed by what she sees before her. Nature is divine – "God is here" –; nature possesses the power to compel Dickinson's awe in a way that a traditional, religious God has not. Indeed, the rapturous love that Dickinson feels and expresses for nature is the rapture of worship:

> These are the days when Birds come back –
> A very few – a Bird or two –
> To take a backward look.
>
> These are the days when skies resume
> The old – old sophistries of June –
> A blue and gold mistake.
>
> Oh fraud that cannot cheat the Bee –
> Almost thy plausibility
> Induces my belief.
>
> Till ranks of seeds their witness bear –
> And softly thro' the altered air
> Hurries a timid leaf.
>
> Oh Sacrament of summer days,
> Oh Last Communion in the Haze –
> Permit a child to join.
>
> Thy sacred emblems to partake –
> Thy consecrated bread to take
> And thine immortal wine!
>
> (*P* 61, no. 130)

This poem describes those early winter days that suggest the return of spring or summer. The reverent, even religious language which Dickinson uses to speak of these days' misleading beauties is remarkable. The beauty of such days tricks a few birds into prematurely returning, while the skies mistakenly "resume the old . . . sophistries of June." It is important to note that the center of faith in this poem is not God, but June. Dickinson draws a parallel between Christ's return and the return of summer; in her view, June's return is more full of promise than the Messiah's. Though the omens of promised June are essentially fraudulent, they are harmless. Unlike the false and unfulfilled promises of a returning Christ, they "cannot cheat the Bee." The promises of spring are not altogether a ruse because they include a reliable "cloud of witnesses" (Hebrews 12:1) that actually produces a summer "leaf." For Dickinson, these beautiful, deceptive days are a "Sacrament of summer days, / [A] Last Communion in the Haze." They are a Eucharist, a Last Supper, a communion in which any "child" can join.[54] The blue and gold sky and the timid leaf are the "sacred emblems" of summer that reassure the viewer that the season of growth will return. Just as Christians are to participate in the bread and wine of communion as a token of Christ's return,[55] Dickinson participates in the "Sacrament" of these late summer days as a sign that this cycle of spring and summer will repeat itself. Nature, not Christ, is Dickinson's source of hope and ecstasy.

The religious devotion that Dickinson felt for life on earth is an important wellspring of her poetry. Rejecting religious dogma, Dickinson embraces sensory truths and the truths of nature's beauty. Her devotion is not to God, her mission not to achieve heaven; instead her loyalties lie with this life and this earth:

> Some keep the Sabbath going to Church –
> I keep it, staying at Home –
> With a Bobolink for a Chorister –
> And an Orchard, for a Dome –
>
> Some keep the Sabbath in Surplice –
> I just wear my Wings –
> And instead of tolling the Bell, for Church,
> Our little Sexton – sings.
>
> God preaches, a noted Clergyman –
> And the sermon is never long,
> So instead of getting to Heaven, at last –
> I'm going, all along.   (*P* 153–4, no. 324)

Dickinson is not interested in organized religion, its requirements, or rituals. She prefers the simple doctrines that nature offers. The warbling of the birds and the humming of the bees are true paradise, constituting sermons more edifying than those of a ponderous preacher. The "Bobolink" and "Orchard" replace the cold music and atmosphere of the choir and cathedral dome. The pomp of the preacher's "Surplice" garment is discarded, and the speaker joins the birds, thus donning a pair of "Wings" more angelic than the white surplice that covers the preacher's heavy black robe. The light and blissful events of nature replace the cold and dark rituals of the church. In contrast to the sexton of the church who "toll[s] the Bell" for church as if it were a funeral service and whose other responsibilities include gravedigging, the "Sexton" bird is full of life and sings a beautiful melody for the poet. Notice that Dickinson does not speak of ringing the bell for church but of tolling it. By invoking the funereal bell toll and the gravedigging sexton, Dickinson aligns the rituals of the church with death. The church's message is death-centered in its emphasis on a life after death. In contrast, Dickinson revels in this life as her way of keeping the "Sabbath." Instead of looking only toward death and the heaven promised after death, she enjoys heaven now; heaven is not a destination after death, it is the process of life itself. Dickinson is "going [to heaven], all along" by drinking in and reverencing this heaven on earth.

The heavenliness of nature was a constant subject for Dickinson's poems. Because she reverenced nature so intensely, Dickinson constantly felt the need to describe and praise nature's beauties in her own poetic hymns.

> "Nature" is what we see –
> The Hill – the Afternoon –
> Squirrel – Eclipse – the Bumble bee –
> Nay – Nature is Heaven –
> Nature is what we hear –
> The Bobolink – the Sea –
> Thunder – the Cricket –
> Nay – Nature is Harmony –
> Nature is what we know –
> Yet have no art to say –
> So impotent Our Wisdom is
> To her Simplicity.   (*P* 332, no. 668)

Once again, Dickinson assigns herself the task of defining nature, even as she claims it is ineffable. Because nature is "what we know – / Yet have no art to say," Dickinson describes it simply with a catalogue; nature is "The Hill," "the Afternoon," a "Squirrel," an "Eclipse," "the Bumble bee," "The Bobolink," "the Sea," "Thunder," and "the Cricket." A squirrel or a bumble bee is as heavenly as an eclipse; a bobolink's song is as powerful as the music of the sea; the chanting of a cricket is as important as the crashing thunder. The great and small are equally important to Dickinson. Even nature in her utmost "Simplicity" is heavenly.

While the Transcendentalists often observed nature to discover metaphors for the soul and to learn eternal truths, Dickinson believed the minutest details of nature were significant in themselves – not as signs or representations of higher truths.[56]

> The Spider holds a Silver Ball
> In unperceived Hands –
> And dancing softly to Himself
> His Yarn of Pearl – unwinds –
>
> He plies from Nought to Nought –
> In unsubstantial Trade –

Supplants our Tapestries with His –
In half the period –

An Hour to rear supreme
His Continents of Light –
Then dangle from the Housewife's Broom –
His Boundaries – forgot –   (*P* 297, no. 605)

For Dickinson, the spider's weaving is so remarkable that it deserves a poem to honor and celebrate its intricacy. Of course, the poem also serves as a warning of temporality, as the spider's handiwork, his "Continents of Light," survives only an hour and soon "dangle from the Housewife's Broom." Similarly, the poet and her woven poems may also be subject to the ravages of time and succeeding generations. But while the spider's work is small and his artistry is soon destroyed by an industrious housewife, the beauty of the pattern he creates is worthy to be remembered in a more permanent, though still fragile, form. The spider's weaving is significant in itself; in essence, it is the same as Dickinson's poetic weavings. Just as Dickinson wrote her poems for herself, the spider weaves a beautiful web as he "dance[es] softly to Himself." (Notice how the "Spider" and the pronouns that refer back to him are capitalized to highlight his importance.) The web is the outward result of an internal music. While both the web and Dickinson's poems might be destroyed by an unimpressed audience, the internal music that created them, life, is worth remembering. Thus, while Dickinson uses nature's images to explore her own life, the natural life that created these images is no less important.

Emily Dickinson found grace not in salvation and religious sacraments but in the sacramental communion she enjoyed with nature: "By carrying the Victorian dictate of feminine receptivity to its extreme, Dickinson discovered what mystics call the joy of cosmic fusion, or being one with the universe."[57] Many of Dickinson's poems record the ecstasy that Dickinson achieved in particularly rich moments of communion with the earth.

The Sun went down – no Man looked on –
The Earth and I, alone,
Were present at the Majesty –
He triumphed, and went on –

The Sun went up – no Man looked on –
The Earth and I and One
A nameless Bird – a Stranger
Were Witness for the Crown –

(*P* 489, no. 1079)

The poem's religious imagery supplants the Christian dogma of salvation and eternal life with an ecstatic moment of communion with the earth. The moment is like a revelation of God's "Majesty" (cf. Revelation 1, 4), but instead of witnessing a vision of God, Dickinson experiences a revelatory vision of the earth. She is not a "Witness for the Crown" like the apostle John was, by beholding a vision of Christ's return and coming reign (Revelation 21), but by participating in the earth's rhythms and observing the sunrise with the earth and a nameless bird, who itself becomes a witness and a saint not of Christ but of the earth. Ecstasy comes for Dickinson not from a religious vision or experience but from a powerful connection with the earth.

Although the harmony that Dickinson feels with nature allows her transcendent moments of communion, her love was not blind to its darker rhythms. For Dickinson, the details of nature are capable of producing not only ecstatic bliss but also heart-wrenching despair. Thus, "a certain Slant of light" could oppress Dickinson with a weight of death:

> There's a certain Slant of light,
> Winter Afternoons –
> That oppresses, like the Heft
> Of Cathedral Tunes –
>
> Heavenly Hurt, it gives us –
> We can find no scar,
> But internal difference,
> Where the Meanings, are –
>
> None may teach it – Any –
> 'Tis the Seal Despair –
> An imperial affliction
> Sent us of the Air –
>
> When it comes, the Landscape listens –
> Shadows – hold their breath –
> When it goes, 'tis like the Distance
> On the look of Death –
>
> (P 118–19, no. 258)

The language used here conveys heaviness, sorrow, confusion: "Hurt," "oppresses," "Heft," "difference," "Despair," "affliction," "Shadows," "Distance," and "Death" are nature's negative influences. The heaviness of religious ritual that Dickinson earlier sought to cast off in her keeping of the Sabbath is now present in nature, whose "certain Slant of light . . . oppresses, like the Heft / Of Cathedral Tunes." The bareness of winter forces Dickinson to contemplate death itself. Nature's mysteries include darkness, at times even cruelty, and Dickinson does not "repress the darker aspects of her vision in order to create the illusion of control."[58] On the contrary, because Dickinson is dedicated to recording every emotion thoroughly, of mapping experience in its entirety, she does not hesitate to contemplate nature's destructive power. "Sometimes she portrayed the negative force in nature as male – a marauding bee who assaults a flower's tranquility, the rapining sun who seduces and then scorches nature's delicate vegetation, or death as the inevitable abductor."[59] However she chose to portray the menacing aspects of nature, Dickinson accepted this dimension as part of life. She avoided a cultish and naïve worship of the earth by recognizing its complexities, and by committing herself not only to the full range of her emotions but to all of nature's displays.

> The Sky is low – the Clouds are mean.
> A Travelling Flake of Snow
> Across a Barn or through a Rut
> Debates if it will go –
>
> A Narrow Wind complains all Day
> How some one treated him
> Nature, like Us is sometimes caught
> Without her Diadem.
>
> (*P* 488, no. 1075)

Written the same year as "The Sun went down," this poem catches nature at her worst. There is nothing uplifting about this mean and petulant winter day, but Dickinson faithfully records what she sees in this brief, but perfect, poem.

Beyond even nature's inglorious moments, Dickinson also confronted nature's threatening power. "Nature could be wantonly destructive as well as awesome or sublime."[60] Dickinson did not ignore nature's tendency to harm as well as protect her creatures.

> Nature – sometimes sears a Sapling –
> Sometimes – scalps a Tree –
> Her Green People recollect it
> When they do not die –
>
> Fainter Leaves – to Further Seasons –
> Dumbly testify –
> We – who have the Souls –
> Die oftener – Not so vitally –
>
> (*P* 148, no. 314)

Dickinson honors nature's capacity for both transcendent sublimity and hor-rible cruelty[61] and accepts its darkness as well as its brilliant illuminations:

> Through fissures in
> Volcanic cloud
> The yellow lightning shone –
> The trees held up
> Their mangled limbs
> Like animals in pain –
>
> (*P* 691, no. 1694)

Dickinson accepted nature's darkness as well as its joys.

The full range of emotion and experience is Dickinson's poetic terrain, which means she had to accept nature and life in its entirety, had to grapple with and accept death, the darkest and most threatening aspect of the cycle of birth, life, death, and dissolution. Because Dickinson recognized that death was as much a part of nature as life and its joys, she thought a great deal about the emotions that the certainty of death produced in her. Indeed, many of Dickinson's best poems are interested in the problem of death, a problem she could never quite solve until she faced it herself.

"A Riddle, at the last": death and immortality

To fully understand Emily Dickinson's attitude toward life one must grapple, as Dickinson herself did, with the problem of death. Death was *the* problem for Dickinson, a riddle she could never solve but which she always explored, even before the deaths of loved ones during the last decade of her life. Because Dickinson's poetry is dedicated to recording the subtle emotions of the moment, her attitude toward death is not consistent from poem to poem. At times, her poems seem to embrace the possibility, even probability, of immortality and an afterlife. Other poems are more depressed and despairing, while still others suggest the poet's resigned acceptance of uncertainty. The poems record the changes in Dickinson's fluctuating emotions. However, there is a persistent thread of mystery, silence, and uncertainty that always surrounds death in her writing. While her culture attempted to make death familiar and even com-fortable, Dickinson undercut sentimental Victorian ideas about death and the afterlife by emphasizing the inherent inscrutability of death. Her project is not necessarily to clarify death but to explore its silence, mystery, and unknowa-bility as well as to record the range of emotions that the frightening mystery of death awakens in the human heart.

The importance of mortality to Dickinson's work is evident in the sheer number of poems and letters that are preoccupied with the subject. The subject index of Johnson's reading edition of Dickinson's poems lists almost 150 poems under the headings of "dead" and "death." Of course, there are also poems listed under "immortality," "resurrection," and "eternity" that likewise discuss death. The word "death" is mentioned in Dickinson's poetry 141 times, following only "day" (232 times), "sun" (170 times), "life" (156 times), and "heaven" (143 times) as the most repeated noun in her poetry.[62] Indeed, some form of the verb *die* appears in more than ninety poems.[63] Death is also an important subject in Dickinson's letters, especially during the last decade of her life when she writes more letters than poems.[64] Surrounded by the deaths of loved ones, "[n]ot only her own bereavements, but those of others, prompted nearly half of the letters [about 300 letters] now available from Dickinson's last decade" alone:[65]

> From her father's sudden death in June 1874, hardly a year was to pass in which Emily Dickinson escaped loss. In the summer of 1875, her mother suffered a paralyzing stroke, and thenceforth required constant care. In 1878 Samuel Bowles died, and in 1879 Charles Wadsworth. Both men had stimulated Dickinson's intellect and thus enabled her art . . . In 1881 came the death of Dr Holland . . . and in 1882 the demise of Mrs Dickinson . . . The unkindest cut of all came in 1883, when Gilbert, aged eight, died suddenly of typhoid fever. Judge Otis Lord, the romantic love of Emily Dickinson's final years, died in March 1884, and in that June she suffered the first full attack of her own fatal disease. In addition to these losses at the marrow of her life, others she had revered as literary friends and models had also died: Mrs Higginson in 1877, George Eliot in 1880, Emerson in 1882, Helen Hunt Jackson in 1885.[66]

These losses notwithstanding, Dickinson's interest in death is not confined to the last decade of her life. On the contrary, in 1852 at the age of twenty-one Dickinson wrote to Jane Humphrey, "I think of the grave very often" (*L* 197, no. 88). Some of her very earliest poems written in 1852–3, though extremely conventional and sentimental, are nonetheless interested in death, resurrection, and eternity (e.g., *P* 5–7, nos. 4 and 5), subjects that repeatedly reappear in Dickinson's poetry and prose for the remainder of her life.

Though Dickinson's fascination with death might seem an abnormal obsession to contemporary readers in a culture that pushes death to the margins of consciousness, such interest was in fact quite commonplace in nineteenth-century Victorian America. Dickinson's desire to know the particulars of her friends' passings (for example when she wrote to Charles Clark asking him to tell her of his brother James' final days (*L* 778, no. 826)) reflects the culture's obsession with deathbed behavior. According to Janet Buell, this interest in deathbed scenes descended from Puritan ideas that "there was no more telling sign of election than a serene deathbed acceptance which served as inspiration and consolation to those left behind"; in fact, in Dickinson's day, Buell points out, "clergymen kept [detailed] records of their parishioners' conduct on leaving this life."[67] Appropriate deathbed behavior, or *ars moriendi*, was a common topic of conversation as well as an important part of sentimental fiction.[68]

Nineteenth-century America's "widespread fascination with death and immortality [was] exemplified by the massive popularity of mourning manuals, the growth of the rural cemetery movement, and the near-meteoric rise of such sanitizing rituals as embalming."[69] Newspapers, periodicals, and sentimental narratives were also filled with constructions of the afterlife as a domestic space that mimicked this life's familial arrangements. According to Maria Farland, "In the popular fictions of Dickinson's era, friends and family would be reunited in snug, heavenly homes complete with elaborate interior decorations and detailed housekeeping regimes"; death was merely "a mild transition whose gentleness provided evidence of God's kindness."[70] Often, death was depicted as a gentle angel, or a lover, conducting the faithful to a blissful new home.[71] Dickinson's interest in death, then, is not macabre but in alignment with her culture. However, Dickinson's depictions of death are much more complicated and stark than conventional representations; she reverses cultural ideas in order to convey her own more complex attitudes toward death and the afterlife.

Emily Dickinson's early letters seem to embrace the sentimental ideas of the afterlife as a reunion of loved ones. For example, in an 1855 letter to Mrs Holland, Dickinson writes: "Thank God there is a world, and that the friends we love dwell forever and ever in a house above. I fear I grow incongruous, but to meet my friends does delight me so that I quite forget time and sense and so forth" (*L* 319, no. 179). However, the sentences preceding these suggest that this exclamation comes from Dickinson's fear that "there is not a world" (319). The possibility that heaven as well as the world may be a mere "dream" complicates Dickinson's seemingly sure insistence on an eternal reunion with friends. In 1856, Dickinson (again to Mrs Holland) expresses her wishes for a heaven:

> My only sketch, profile, of Heaven is a large, blue sky, bluer and larger than the *biggest* I have seen in June, and in it are my friends – all of them – every one of them – those who are with me now, and those who were "parted" as we walked, and "snatched up to Heaven."
>
> (*L* 329, no. 185)

Since Dickinson's emotional investment in this life was so intense, it is not surprising that in this letter she hopes for a future world that is a potential extension of what she already has and loves – friends, family, and nature. However, her skepticism surfaces again in the letter when Dickinson tells Mrs Holland, "[I]f God had been here this summer, and seen the things that *I* have seen – I guess that He would think His Paradise superfluous. Don't tell Him, for the world, though, for after all He's said about it, I should like to see what He *was* building for us, with no hammer, and no stone, and no journeyman either." The playful, mocking tone again registers her disbelief in the heaven that God has promised, the paradise "not made with hands, eternal in the heavens" (II Corinthians 5:1). In an 1858 letter to the Hollands, Dickinson's uncertainty about death creates, but does not answer, questions:

> Good-night! I can't stay any longer in a world of death. Austin is ill of fever. I buried my garden last week – our man, Dick, lost a little girl through the scarlet fever. I thought perhaps that *you* were dead, and not knowing the sexton's address, interrogate the daisies. Ah! dainty – dainty Death! Ah! democratic Death! Grasping the proudest zinnia from my purple garden, – then deep to his bosom calling the serf's child!
>
> Say, is he everywhere? Where shall I hide my things? Who is alive? The woods are dead. Is Mrs. H. alive? Annie and Katie – are they below, or received to nowhere?   (*L* 341, no. 195)

Here, Dickinson's depiction of death undercuts sentimental notions of death's gentleness with darker and more threatening images of death's mystery. While she calls death "dainty" and draws on biblical and religious images of heaven as a gentle calling to Christ's bosom, she also emphasizes the physical grave in her remarks on "the sexton's address" and the daisies that spring from graves "below."

The silence of the grave provides no answers for Dickinson's questions as she struggles to make a connection between the cycles of nature and the deaths of those around her. Her worries are never completely soothed by her culture's expressions of hope: "That *Bareheaded life* – under the grass – worries one like a Wasp" (*L* 364, no. 220). Ultimately, she fears that to die is to be "received to nowhere" rather than to ascend to a fatherly embrace. Thus, in a much later letter expressing her deep grief at Judge Lord's death, even as Dickinson recounts his seemingly peaceful, sentimental passing, she quickly follows with an expression of uncertainty: "Dear Mr. Lord has left us – After a brief unconsciousness, a Sleep that ended with a smile, so his Nieces tell us, he hastened away, 'seen,' we trust, 'of Angels' – 'Who knows that secret deep' – 'Alas, not I –'" (*L* 816, no. 890). Even as Dickinson employs sentimental images to represent death, she undercuts them with questions and uncertainties. Dickinson is haunted by the unknowability of death's "secret deep."

Some of Dickinson's most famous and most powerful poems turn on the connections they make with reversals of sentimental notions of death and immortality. While sentimental fictions were designed to cover death's fearful darkness with soft language and familiar images that render death less frightening, Dickinson's poems often strip death of such reassuring language, highlighting instead its mystery and uncertainty. Dickinson's extremely famous poem "Because I could not stop for Death" draws on the sentimental idea of death as a gentle lover escorting his love to a new and blissful home.[72]

> Because I could not stop for Death
> He kindly stopped for me –
> The Carriage held but just Ourselves –
> And Immortality.
>
> We slowly drove – He knew no haste
> And I had put away
> My labor and my leisure too,
> For His Civility –
>
> We passed the School, where Children strove
> At Recess – in the Ring –
> We passed the Fields of Gazing Grain –
> We passed the Setting Sun –
>
> Or rather – He passed Us –
> The Dews drew quivering and chill –
> For only Gossamer, my Gown –
> My Tippet – only Tulle –
>
> We paused before a House that seemed
> A Swelling of the Ground –
> The Roof was scarcely visible –
> The Cornice – in the Ground –
>
> Since then – 'tis Centuries – and yet
> Feels shorter than the Day
> I first surmised the Horses' Heads
> Were toward Eternity –   (*P* 350, no. 712)

The motif of death as a courtly lover is highlighted in the poem's first three stanzas. Death here is "kindly" and offers the narrator a smooth journey to the afterlife. The journey is slow, not frighteningly hasty or bumpy, and death is full of chivalric "Civility." The journey includes familiar scenes as the carriage glides past the school and fields. However, the fourth stanza brings an abrupt turn to the poem. In the first three stanzas, the spatial coordinates of the poem are clear and consistent. The carriage journeys straight away from the home and town, eventually passing "the Setting Sun." However, when the narrator suddenly adds, "Or rather – He passed Us –," the journey's progress suddenly becomes confusing. This abrupt turn in the poem flags a movement away from the sentimental idea of death as an easy spiritual journey. Instead of moving smoothly past the setting sun to the heavens, the journey ends rather abruptly and the scene becomes threatening. The poem has quickly moved from the positive image of "the Fields of Gazing Grain" to the darker image of the "Dews . . . quivering and chill" that threaten a vulnerable body clad with "*only* Gossamer" and "*only* Tulle." The journey ends not with the arrival at a heavenly home, but in the buried and suffocating home "in the Ground" – the physical grave. The carriage that seemed so comfortable in the first half of the poem is not a chariot that transports a soul to an afterlife but a hearse transporting a body to the cemetery. "Eternity" seems nothing more than "Centuries" of physical decay in the earth that feel shorter than "the Day" when the narrator first noticed she was on her way to death. This poem's last stanza also suggests that true eternity lies in the single day in which we recognize death and thus capitalize on the present moment, which is itself infinite.[73]

"Death is a supple Suitor" takes an even darker view of the sentimental death-as-lover motif.

> Death is the supple Suitor
> That wins at last –
> It is a stealthy Wooing
> Conducted first
> By pallid innuendoes
> And dim approach
> But brave at last with Bugles
> And a bisected Coach
> It bears away in triumph
> To Troth unknown
> And Kindred as responsive
> As Porcelain.
>
> (*P* 614, no. 1445)

This poem's vision of the afterlife is not one of reunion at the warm and happy domestic hearth that the culture usually propounded. Death as suitor is not a positive and gentle image here, but a "stealthy" and even violating danger. There is no happy reunion with friends and family. Here we have only the coldness and stillness of the corpse and the mausoleum.

Again and again, Dickinson's poems undercut sentimental ideas of death. Instead of recording a comforting and inspiring deathbed scene in which the dying individual experiences a religious revelation and a peaceful conclusion to mortal life, Dickinson imagines dying as anticlimactic in "I heard a Fly buzz – when I died –."

> I heard a Fly buzz – when I died –
> The Stillness in the Room
> Was Like the Stillness in the Air –
> Between the Heaves of Storm –
>
> The Eyes around – had wrung them dry –
> And Breaths were gathering firm
> For that last Onset – when the King
> Be witnessed – in the Room –
>
> I willed away my Keepsakes – Signed Away
> What portion of me be
> Assignable – and then it was
> There interposed a Fly –
>
> With Blue – uncertain stumbling Buzz –
> Between the light – and me –
> And then the Windows failed – and then
> I could not see to see –
>
> (*P* 223–4, no. 465)

In this poem, the speaker, now a corpse, and the friends gathered round are trying to enact a sentimental deathbed scene. The faces of loved ones brace for the final moments, possessions and keepsakes are willed away, the last words are spoken, and the arrival of "the King" who will lead the dying to heaven is anticipated. But instead of being gently led by Christ, a common fly interposes, undercutting the solemnity of the scene: the speaker sees a fly, and then the light suddenly fails and death takes over. Dickinson highlights the isolation of death and cuts the speaker off from the group gathered round by using dashes to cut off and isolate the "me" of the poem in the last stanza. There is no gentle passage into death, only an abrupt, awkward, and isolating end that seems as "uncertain" and "stumbling" as the flight of the fly.

For Dickinson, death is not the known, mappable terrain of Victorian narratives but an ultimately impenetrable region: "Dust is the only Secret – / Death, the only One / You cannot find out all about" (*P* 72, no. 153). The silence of the grave prohibits any certainty about life after death. In "I felt a Funeral, in my Brain," the speaking corpse is silenced before it can give any hints about life after death:

I felt a Funeral, in my Brain,
And Mourners to and fro
Kept treading – treading – till it seemed
That Sense was breaking through –

And when they all were seated,
A Service, like a Drum –
Kept beating – beating – till I thought
My Mind was going numb –

And then I heard them lift a Box
And creak across my Soul
With those same Boots of Lead, again,
Then Space – began to toll,

As all the Heavens were a Bell,
And Being, but an Ear,
And I, and Silence, some strange Race
Wrecked, solitary, here –

And then a Plank in Reason, broke,
And I dropped down, and down –
And hit a World, at every plunge,
And Finished knowing – then –

(*P* 128–9, no. 280)

At death, "Being" may become an "Ear," but it has no voice to tell what it hears. Death may result in hyper-self-consciousness, but nothing can be communicated. Death is a place of "I, and Silence"; the speaker "drop[s] down, and down" into death and "Finishe[s] knowing – then –." The poem feels unfinished because the truth of what death is cannot be communicated. Death is unknowable except to the dead, who are of course silent and probably not sentient in Dickinson's view.[74]

The silence and mystery of the grave are constants in Dickinson's writings even when she tries to hope that there is an afterlife or some kind of reunion of loved ones. "This World is not Conclusion" (*P* 243, no. 501) while claiming at its beginning that there is another world beyond this one, focuses more on the mystery of death than the certainty of afterlife:

This World is not Conclusion.
A Species stands beyond –
Invisible, as Music –
But positive, as Sound –
It beckons, and it baffles –

Philosophy – don't know –
And through a Riddle, at the last –
Sagacity, must go –
To guess it, puzzles scholars –
To gain it, Men have borne
Contempt of Generations
And Crucifixion, shown –
Faith slips – and laughs, and rallies –
Blushes, if any see –
Plucks at a twig of Evidence –
And asks a Vane, the way –
Much Gesture, from the Pulpit –
Strong Hallelujahs roll –
Narcotics cannot still the Tooth
That nibbles at the soul –

Like "Music," immortality "baffles" the poet because no language clarifies its meaning. Death is a "Riddle" that "puzzles scholars" but which "at the last" everyone must pass through in order to reach "Sagacity." Death is, as Dickinson calls it in another poem, a "bland uncertainty" (*P* 674, no. 1646). The best one can do is imagine the afterlife because death is "Further than Guess can gallop / Further than Riddle ride" (*P* 445, no. 949). Dickinson cleverly uses a pun to say that trying to understand death is as vain as asking "a Vane, the way." All the thundering pronouncements from the pulpit cannot nullify the grave's silence or erase the gnawing uncertainty about death and eternity.

In discussing her father's death in a letter to Higginson (1874), Dickinson writes, "I am glad there is Immortality – but would have tested it myself – before entrusting him" (*L* 528, no. 418). Dickinson's desire to locate her father in "Immortality" is complicated by its uncertainty and mystery. In her letter to Susan after Gilbert's death (*L* 799, no. 868), Dickinson grounds much of her consolation in Gilbert's earthly life, while representing his death as an initiation into a secret: "The Vision of Immortal Life has been fulfilled – How simply at last the Fathom comes! . . . Gilbert rejoiced in Secrets – His Life was panting with them . . . Now my ascended Playmate must instruct *me*. Show us, prattling Preceptor, but the way to thee!" Dickinson employs sentimental ideas about death to console her friend by describing Gilbert's death as an ascension to the heavens, but she also emphasizes the mystery, "the Fathom" of death that Gilbert has now discovered. The rest of her letter focuses on his earthly life and then once again returns to the essential mystery of death in its enclosed poem: "Pass to thy Rendezvous of Light, / Pangless except for us – / Who slowly ford the Mystery / Which thou hast leaped across." Dickinson registers her uncertainty about an afterlife even more vividly in her description of Gilbert's last moments to Mrs Holland: "he ran to the little Grave at his Grandparent's feet – All this and more, though *is* there more? More than Love and Death? Then tell me it's name!" (*L* 803, no. 873). The silence of the grave resists any elucidation of its secret.

Ultimately, Dickinson is not committed to sanitizing death, though she does, at times, employ sentimental conventions in order to console others. On the contrary, her project is one of recording. Embracing life in all its variations, even its most painful, Dickinson explores death as one of life's most poignant experiences. Her ability to describe the pain, as well as anger, one feels after the death of a loved one draws on her own intense feelings of grief:

> After great pain, a formal feeling comes –
> The Nerves sit ceremonious, like Tombs –
> The stiff Heart questions was it He, that bore,
> And Yesterday, or Centuries before?
>
> The Feet, mechanical, go round –
> Of Ground, or Air, or Ought –
> A Wooden way
> Regardless grown,
> A Quartz contentment, like a stone –
>
> This is the Hour of Lead –
> Remembered, if outlived,
> As Freezing persons, recollect the Snow –
> First – Chill – then Stupor – then the letting go –
>
> (*P* 162, no. 341)

Dickinson describes the way a loved one's death leaves an individual empty, cold, almost dead themselves, moving mechanically through the world without any real sense of the life that moves around them. The death of a loved one creates an emptiness in the mourner that is not only a miniature death of the self, but also a preview of the mourner's own death. The heavy stupor that is one of the stages of grief may be outlived, but it is always remembered as a pall cast on one's own life.

Recording momentary feelings allows Dickinson to capture not just the intense pain, but the anger and guilt that accompany grief:

> How dare the robins sing,
> When men and women hear
> Who since they went to their account
> Have settled with the year! –

> Paid all that life had earned
> In one consummate bill,
> And now, what life or death can do
> Is immaterial.   (*P* 700, no. 1724)

The robin's song is an insult to the dead's memory, and the guilt of continuing to live and enjoy the robin's song when the dead cannot oppresses the mourner. Dickinson explores the complex emotions involved in mourning, while also imagining death from the perspective of the dying person.

For Dickinson, death is the most intense of moments, the moment of profound meaning between friends ("Parting is all we know of heaven, / And all we need of hell" (*P* 703, no. 1732)) but also a moment with the potential for self-discovery, a journey into a terrifying hyper-self-consciousness.

> This Consciousness that is aware
> Of Neighbors and the Sun
> Will be the one aware of Death
> And that itself alone
>
> Is traversing the interval
> Experience between
> And most profound experiment
> Appointed unto Men –
>
> How adequate unto itself
> Its properties shall be
> Itself unto itself and none
> Shall make discovery.
>
> Adventure most unto itself
> The Soul condemned to be –
> Attended by a single Hound
> Its own identity.
>   (*P* 399, no. 822)

Death is still the unknown, as always in Dickinson; here she imagines it as a journey into oneself, a journey of self-discovery that may possibly become a hunt in which one is hounded by one's own identity. As always, however, death is the "most profound experiment / Appointed unto Men."

Whether in moments of hope, despair, acceptance, or anger, Dickinson always registers the fundamental inscrutability of death. She explores and imagines death, not to uncover any certainty about death and immortality, but to grapple with its mystery and uncertainty. Dickinson was never able to solve death's "riddle," but ultimately, for Dickinson, the apparent finality of death is what gives meaning to life. Anticipating Wallace Stevens' sentiment that "death is the mother of beauty," Dickinson makes clear that one's appreciation of life is affected by the ability to accept and remember the reality of death.[75]

> The Admirations – and Contempts – of time –
> Show justest – through an Open Tomb –
> The Dying – as it were a Height
> Reorganizes Estimate
> And what We saw not
> We distinguish clear –
> And mostly – see not
> What We saw before –
>
> 'Tis compound Vision –
> Light – enabling Light –
> The Finite – furnished
> With the Infinite –
> Convex – and Concave Witness –
> Back – toward Time –
> And forward –
> Toward the God of Him –   (*P* 428, no. 906)

The certainty of death gives a new perspective on life – a "compound Vision" that illuminates through contrast and encompasses presence and absence, past and future, "Convex" and "Concave." Such perspective reorganizes the "Estimate" of time and discovers eternity in the present moment. This brief life is the "single Dram of Heaven" that the soul is given (*P* 700, no. 1725); its briefness does not take away from its heavenliness, but intensifies it. Eternity for Dickinson is not an endless extension of literal days, or a physical place, but a perspective of time that creates a heightened appreciation of the infinite potential of the moment:

> The Blunder is in estimate.
> Eternity is there
> We say, as of a Station –
> Meanwhile he is so near
> He joins me in my Ramble –
> Divides abode with me –
> No Friend have I that so persists
> As this Eternity
>   (*P* 687–8, no. 1684)

Any linear measurement of time – to "estimate" – is a blunder. Eternity exists in the unfolding moment of the present, not as a location in a distant heaven.

"I find ecstasy in living," Dickinson once said, "– the mere sense of living is joy enough" (*L* 474, no. 342a). The "ecstasy of living," the "omnipotence" that Dickinson feels in being "alive," is "enough" to make this existence profoundly worthwhile, even if there is no existence after death (*P* 335, no. 677).

Thus, for Dickinson, one's legacy ultimately lies in the ability to live fully in the present and to bequeath a legacy of self to loved ones. Dickinson's bequest is the poetry that records her own attempts to understand and appreciate each individual moment. In the effort to achieve "circumference," her poems offer a wide range of sometimes contradictory perspectives that depend upon the moment in which she wrote. Sometimes the poems plunge into dangerous self-reflection or despair. Sometimes they embrace a moment of transcendence and ecstasy. Dickinson's poems map the flux and changes of human experience. They are the legacy of a life lived with full consciousness and self-awareness.

Chapter 4

Reception

"The Auction Of the Mind": publication history   *110*
Editing the poems and letters   *117*
Early reception   *121*
New Criticism   *123*
Dickinson's legacy today   *128*

The poems and letters of Emily Dickinson that survive today are the result of relatives who saved her work, editors who published it, critics who studied it, and generations of readers who continue to celebrate it. In fact, the history of how Dickinson's works were published and received is just as exciting, mysterious, and controversial as the poems themselves. To understand the poems today, it is useful to begin with the print history of her work and Dickinson's own reservations about publication.

After Emily Dickinson's death, Lavinia Dickinson inherited the painful task of sorting through her sister's possessions and cleaning out the room that had enclosed her for many years. Dickinson asked for her notes and correspondence to be destroyed after her death, so Lavinia dutifully collected papers in preparation for burning. However, as she opened desk drawers and boxes, Lavinia stumbled across a cache of over 1,700 poems, an astonishing collection that no one knew existed.[1] Despite her sister's wishes, Lavinia knew the poems were too precious and important to consign to the fire. She saved the poems, making a vow to have them published. Without Lavinia's dedication to her sister's poetry, the life's work of one of America's most important poets would have vanished. However, through publication, Dickinson's private poems and letters were exposed to public scrutiny and judgment for appreciation or censure.

"The Auction Of the Mind": publication history

The manuscripts that survive today are difficult to label. Dickinson excelled at creating chimera – papers that have the look of letters but the sound and rhythm of poems, or poems that read as straightforward correspondence. Her letters often utilized alliteration, assonance, and rhyme, even when written as mere newsletters and thank-you notes. Sometimes the poems in the fascicles appear in the form of letters sent to different people, each with slight variations. Dickinson clearly liked to blur boundaries and saw no reason to compartmentalize her writing. The fact that she wrote letters to Sue that were small enough to fit in a dress pocket probably means that she kept her drafts close to her body, working and reworking them throughout the day.[2]

The difficulty in classifying her manuscripts is only one of the factors that has affected Dickinson's publication history. Perhaps for Dickinson more than any other American poet, the issue of publication is thickly interwoven with discussions of biography, history, aesthetics, and interpretation. What constitutes a poem? When can a letter be called a poem, or a poem a letter? How are different types of writing defined? How important are characteristics of handwriting or stray pencil marks? These are some of the many questions that editors and readers of Dickinson's poetry must answer. Only a few of Dickinson's poems were published during her lifetime, and there is much debate over whether Dickinson chose to submit and publish even those poems, or whether they were surreptitiously published by friends and fans. Regardless of how the poems ended up in the hands of editors, each subsequent editor, challenged by Dickinson's unusual and rebellious verse, altered the poems in some fashion to make the works more appealing to their own tastes and the public's expectations.

The literary tastes of Dickinson's lifetime placed a strong emphasis on form, content, and propriety. A literary work was expected to be written in the form that best suited its subject, with common signposts such as titles, chapters, stanzas, and other markers that were familiar to all readers. In terms of poetry, readers preferred predictable rhyme schemes and even, unaltered meter. Although Dickinson's juvenile manuscripts rely on these established forms, as she matured as a writer she utilized them less and less, striking out on her own territory: irregular use of capitalization and punctuation, "slant" or off-rhyme, varied or broken meter, and intricately knotted meaning.

Dickinson wrote poems to please herself and a select audience of friends and relatives. Unfettered by the economic and aesthetic demands of publishing, she could create dangerous, provocative, rebellious, cryptic, heretical, and erotic poems without fear of public censure or condemnation. She could also break standard rules of grammar, punctuation, rhyme, and meter. Because many of her poems were intended for a specific person, Dickinson could also include inside jokes and subtle, intimate references in her poems that are lost on a large reading public. In many ways, Emily Dickinson's steadfast refusal to publish her work allowed her the freedom to create. However, the challenge of studying poetry that was never published is that it is very difficult to discern what the author originally wrote and intended, and what was changed by subsequent editors.

The first publication of Dickinson's poetry occurred in 1850, when she was nineteen years old and the Amherst College *Indicator* published a valentine poem. This early poem addresses love, death, nature, immortality, and heaven – themes which she would continue to broaden and deepen throughout her life. The poem chronicles how "All things do go a courting" and presents a catalogue of romantic pairings, including Adam and Eve, the moon and the sun, and the bee and the flower. Most of the poem presents clichéd, traditional images of romantic coupling that would have been standard fare for a teenage girl in the 1850s. However, one strikingly dark, distinct line stands out among all of the romantic platitudes. Within the list of couplings, Dickinson includes, "The *worm* doth woo the *mortal*, death claims a living bride" (*P* 3, no. 1). Suddenly, what appears to be a typical, light-hearted valentine surprises its readers with images that pair marriage with death. This poem is a harbinger of the more mature, finely tuned, and carefully wrought Dickinson poems to come.

Just after Valentine's Day two years later, on 20 February 1852, the *Springfield Daily Republican* printed another Dickinson poem. Like the first valentine poem, "Sic transit gloria mundi" refers to Adam, bees, and celestial bodies. Only the published version of this poem exists, so modern readers cannot compare the final version with Dickinson's handwritten one. However, the published poem is organized into quatrains (four-line stanzas), whereas Dickinson's handwritten poems are often organized into eight-line stanzas. The published version also uses many semicolons, which Dickinson herself did not use. Overall, the published version of "Sic transit gloria mundi" simply looks too *neat* to be the work of a poet who constantly pushed the boundaries of punctuation, rhyme, grammar, and meaning.

The disjunction between the qualities of Dickinson's handwritten manuscripts and the structure of the published poems continued in 1861 with the publication of "I taste a liquour never brewed" (*P* 98–9, no. 214). In fact, the editors of this poem actually rewrote two of Dickinson's lines in order to create perfect rhymes. One version of the poem read:

> I taste a liquor never brewed –
> From Tankards scooped in Pearl –
> Not all the Vats upon the Rhine
> Yield such an Alcohol!
>
> Inebriate of Air – am I –
> And Debauchee of Dew –
> Reeling – thro endless summer days –
> From inns of Molten Blue –

When "Landlords" turn the drunken Bee
Out of the Foxglove's door –
When Butterflies – renounce their "drams" –
I shall but drink the more!

Till Seraphs swing their snowy Hats –
And Saints – to windows run –
To see the little Tippler
Leaning against the – Sun –

(*P* 98–9, no. 214)

In this version, Dickinson rhymes the second and fourth lines of each quatrain (Pearl / Alcohol, Dew / Blue, door / more, run / Sun). However, "Pearl" and "Alcohol" are "slant" or "near" rhymes rather than true rhymes. Clearly, she had the technical skill to choose a true rhyme, but instead sacrificed rhyme in order to achieve an interesting juxtaposition between a naturally occurring item found in the ocean and a man-made liquid found on land. Emily Dickinson's editors, however, could not stand to leave the imperfect rhyme and replaced "Alcohol." Not only did this action change the meaning, it also appeared to be a type of moral editing, since the temperance movement in America labeled the consumption of alcohol a sin. The editors also titled the poem "The May-Wine," probably to suit its May publication. Adding titles, replacing capital letters with lowercase type, and regularizing rhyme were all common editorial practices.

In 1862, the thirty-one-year-old Dickinson wrote a letter to her literary mentor, Thomas Wentworth Higginson, regarding publication. Although Higginson clearly had Dickinson's eventual publication in mind, she writes, "I smile when you suggest that I delay 'to publish' – that being foreign to my thought, as Firmament to Fin –" (*L* 408, no. 265). Indeed, in the foreign world of publishing, Dickinson would have been a fish out of water.

Perhaps the most egregious editing of a published poem during Dickinson's lifetime occurred on yet another Valentine's Day, this time in 1866, when "A narrow Fellow in the Grass" was published in the *Springfield Daily* and *Weekly Republican*:

A narrow Fellow in the Grass
Occasionally rides –
You may have met Him – did you not
His notice sudden is –

The Grass divides as with a Comb –
A spotted shaft is seen –
And then it closes at your feet
And opens further on –

He likes a Boggy Acre
A Floor too cool for Corn –
Yet when a Boy, and Barefoot –
I more than once at Noon
Have passed, I thought, a Whip lash
Unbraiding in the Sun
When stooping to secure it
It wrinkled, and was gone –

Several of Nature's People
I know, and they know me –
I feel for them a transport
Of cordiality –

But never met this Fellow
Attended, or alone
Without a tighter breathing
And Zero at the Bone –

(*P* 459–60, no. 986)

Part of the playfulness of this poem is the riddle at its heart. Who is this strange, "narrow Fellow" with a predilection for boggy acres? Dickinson purposely misleads her audience, playing with anthropomorphism, describing the snake in human terms ("rides," "Him," one of "Nature's People," "Attended, or alone") while slowly revealing hints as to the fellow's true nature ("spotted shaft," "a Whip lash / Unbraiding," "wrinkled"). However, Dickinson's carefully measured and playful riddle was completely undermined by editor Samuel Bowles, who published the poem as "The Snake," giving away the central riddle from the very start.

In addition to the title, Bowles clumped Dickinson's stanzas together, making them into three tidy stanzas of eight lines each. This forces the poem to be read much more quickly, losing some of the playful pauses in the original. In reading Dickinson's version, one can see how the stanzas wriggle down the page in short fits and starts, aided by stanza breaks and dashes which read as if thoughts were cut off by the path of a startled snake. Bowles also added a comma to the end of the third line, forcing a pause in the reading. Another change occurred in the fourth line, "His notice sudden is –." The editor replaced "sudden" with "instant." This change alters the sound level of the line, which becomes heavy with short "i" and "s" sounds – h*is*, not*ice*, *instant*, *is*. Although one might argue that this change introduces a snake's hiss, it also removes connotations from the original word. For example, "sudden" often implies "startling," which would fit with finding a snake crossing one's path. These may seem like relatively innocuous changes to many readers. However, to the woman who dedicated her life to crafting poetry, they were a great injustice.

After seeing the publication of her poem and the changes Bowles had made, Dickinson was livid. She sent a newspaper clipping of the poem to Thomas Wentworth Higginson and wrote: "Lest you meet my Snake and suppose I deceive it was robbed of me – defeated too of the third line by the punctuation. The third and fourth were one – I had told you I did not print – I feared you might think me ostensible" (*L* 450, no. 316). Dickinson's idiosyncratic use of capitalization, rhyme, and punctuation may seem capricious or unintentional to modern readers. However, her anger over even relatively small changes to "A narrow Fellow in the Grass" demonstrates that even simple marks on the page were important, deliberate, aesthetic choices made by Dickinson.

Although Dickinson was clear about her resistance to publication, many of her literary friends begged her for poems. Among the most tenacious was Helen Hunt Jackson. "You are a great poet – and it is wrong to the day you live in, that you will not sing aloud," Jackson wrote to Dickinson (*L* 545, no. 444a). Jackson also sent Dickinson a note about an upcoming Roberts Brothers' project, a No Name volume of verse. She pleaded with Dickinson to submit. Whether Dickinson consented or whether Jackson took liberties, Dickinson's "Success is counted sweetest" was published anonymously in the volume. *A Masque of Poets*, edited by Thomas Niles and published in 1878, is a clever collection of anonymous poems intended to tease readers into guessing the true identities of the authors. Many readers thought that Dickinson's poem was written by Ralph Waldo Emerson, which is interesting given both poets' connections to nature and Transcendentalism. Like the editors before and after him, Niles felt dissatisfied with Dickinson's original poem and made textual changes to it without the author's knowledge or consent.

These few forays into publication cemented in Dickinson's mind the problems with formal publication and her own preference for circulating poems exclusively among her friends. A wonderfully self-reflexive poem that is often cited when describing Dickinson's aversion to formal publishing is the poem "Publication – is the Auction":

> Publication – is the Auction
> Of the Mind of Man –
> Poverty – be justifying
> For so foul a thing
>
> Possibly – but We – would rather
> From Our Garret go
> White – Unto the White Creator –
> Than invest – Our Snow –

> Thought belong to Him who gave it –
> Then – to Him Who bear
> Its Corporeal illustration – Sell
> The Royal Air –
>
> In the Parcel – Be the Merchant
> Of the Heavenly Grace –
> But reduce no Human Spirit
> To Disgrace of Price –
>
>   (*P* 348–9, no. 709)

Written around 1863, after the editorial tampering of "A narrow Fellow in the Grass," this poem draws Dickinson's line in the publication sand. She uses the term "Auction," which in the 1860s would have been closely associated with slavery, to describe the process of literary publication. To publish one's work is to put a price on one's mind, to put one's soul on the auction block. Throughout the poem, Dickinson thrusts gentle words such as "Snow," "Grace," "Air," and "Spirit" against cold, hard, economical terms such as "Auction," "Poverty," "invest," "Sell," and "Price." In doing so, she forces the reader to feel the tension between fragile creativity, which must be nurtured and protected, and ruthless publication, which will sacrifice everything to make the bottom line. Dickinson's distaste for publication aligns with a larger concern about "a society dominated by excessive competition and the profit motive."[3] Like Thoreau, Emerson, and Whitman, Dickinson viewed the "progress" around her as a "narrowing of consciousness, not to mention conscience."[4]

In addition to her fears of editorial tampering and ascribing a price tag to creativity, Dickinson enjoyed her hard-won anonymity and the freedom it gave her. In 1861, when Dickinson was thirty years old, she wrote a deceptively childlike poem which playfully articulates her delight in being a "Nobody" and her desire to avoid being made "public," to protect her name from being mechanically reproduced over and over like an advertisement:

> I'm Nobody! Who are you?
> Are you – Nobody – Too?
> Then there's a pair of us!
> Don't tell! they'd advertise – you know!
>
> How dreary – to be – Somebody!
> How public – like a Frog –
> To tell one's name – the livelong June –
> To an admiring Bog!
>
>   (*P* 133, no. 288)

This poem, arguably one of Dickinson's most cherished, celebrates private individualism and friendship. Although the speaker is considered a "Nobody," she is not completely alone, but sharing herself as part of a pair. The "Somebody," whose name is known, whose work is published, receives admiration. But what good is admiration, Dickinson asks, if it comes from a swamp? Reading the poem, one can almost envision a best-selling author, plump with self-importance, sitting high on a lily pad, croaking away.

Dickinson's concerns over ownership, either of ideas, poetry, or people, occur in many of her poems like "I am afraid to own a Body" (1866) (*P* 493–4, no. 1090). As in "Publication – is the Auction," Dickinson incorporates financial terms such as "Property," "Possession," "Estate," and "Heir," to describe the personal and religious, the "Body" and "Soul." In an interesting twist, the issues raised by "I am afraid to own a Body" tie in with Lavinia Dickinson's situation after her sister's death. This "unsuspecting Heir" stumbled across "Profound – precarious Property" (*P* 493–4, no. 1090) and had no choice but to save it. In that choice, Lavinia began a new phase of publication for Dickinson's work.

Editing the poems and letters

Assembling the poems was a monumental task. Papers were bundled, loose, boxed, pinned, stitched, collected, and folded. Even the assortment of surfaces was daunting; they included "a large accumulation of drafts pencilled on scraps of stationery, notepaper, or wrapping paper, on discarded letters, envelopes, Commencement programs for Massachusetts Agricultural College, advertising circulars, and the like."[5] On top of the sheer number of poems, the documents themselves were faded, folded, and often physically compromised. In addition, the facts that Dickinson wrote at night, used a pencil, and had failing eyesight make the physical appearance of the texts unreliable. The penciled words were light, small, and difficult to decipher. The handwritten nature of the punctuation proved an especial challenge. Were the different lengths of dashes intended to have different meanings, or were they indications of Dickinson's tiredness, light source, or writing whim? The editor would have to decide which letters were capitalized and which punctuation marks were intended.

These decisions might seem minor, but in fact they were integral to Dickinson's art. A typical Dickinson poem is characterized by her use of dashes, odd capitalization, and impenetrable description. Many dissertations, articles, and book chapters have been written about the dash in particular. Scholars have also tried to find patterns in her capitalization. Dickinson's idiosyncratic capitalization, like her use of the dash, may simply have been the best form for what she was trying to express. Although she frequently capitalized nouns, she did not do it exclusively. It is also difficult to distinguish between her uppercase and lowercase letters in the manuscripts, and there is great variation among the letter sizes overall. Capitals often appear at the beginning of lines of poetry, but just as often may appear anywhere else in the line. Some scholars have argued that the capitalization is purely random or accidental. However, given Dickinson's attention to detail, this is unlikely. The capitalization may have been a personal quirk, as various capitals appear in letters, notes, and recipes. Whether they are used for emphasis, pause devices, personification, or some other effect, each editor has had to make choices about the capitals in Dickinson's writing.

Turning Dickinson's handwritten words into typewritten script was much more difficult than it might seem. Her writing and symbols had to be interpreted, translated, and adapted to type. As the adage goes, "something is always lost in translation," and each editor who approached Dickinson's letters and poems had to decide which elements, either the placement of the words on the page, the capitalization, the length of dashes and other punctuation, word variations or even the misspellings, to sacrifice in order to create a clean, readable copy for mass production. It is important to remember that publishing Dickinson's work was a process of adaptation.

Originally, Lavinia took the manuscripts to Susan Dickinson for organization and preparation for publication. However, after two years with the stacks of beguiling, confounding, and perplexing poems, Sue had made no firm progress toward publication. Frustrated, Lavinia took the poems back. She wanted to find someone who was highly motivated, well connected, and able to take charge of the project. The next likely candidate was close family friend Mabel Loomis Todd. Todd helped organize and group the material, then enlisted Dickinson's former Preceptor, Thomas Wentworth Higginson. Together, Todd and Higginson edited the poems to regularize their capitalization, punctuation, lineation, and rhyme in order to align them with nineteenth-century poetic standards. The stunning collection of poems and notes that Lavinia found defied description; there were no words to adequately categorize the various types of writing. In fact, Mabel Loomis Todd applied a term from biology, *fascicle*, to describe the hand-sewn packets of poetry. A fascicle is "a cluster of leaves or flowers with very short stalks growing closely together at the base."[6] It was an appropriately organic term for a poet captivated by flowers and nature. Like the irregular petal clusters bursting from a peony, Dickinson's fascicle poems shared similar roots but were clustered in no easily discernible pattern.[7] Editors would have to first acknowledge the importance of the original pattern before they could strive to replicate it. Instead, Dickinson's first editors unthreaded the fascicles and mixed the order of all the poems.

The first volume of Dickinson's work, *Poems*, was published in Boston in 1890. Todd was publicity-savvy about promoting the new book, and "contacted William Dean Howells, whose prestige, interest in New England manners, and long track record of welcoming brilliant newcomers made him a useful ally."[8] The collection was a success and by 1892 it had gone into eleven editions. They followed the publication with *Poems: Second Series* in 1891 and *Poems: Third Series* in 1896. The success of the poems led Todd to consider editing and publishing the remaining Dickinson letters as well. However, to protect the privacy of the Dickinson family, especially to suppress gossip about Dickinson's love affairs and Austin's infidelity, Todd did a great deal of editing. The first edition of the letters was published in 1894.

The personal friction between Susan and her husband's mistress greatly affected the early publication of Dickinson's work. Because individual letters and poems were held separately by the two camps, no single edition of Dickinson's writing was complete. In fact, a dispute over ownership of the works led both sides to court. Dickinson's niece, Martha Dickinson Bianchi, entered into the publication fray as well, including poems kept by her mother (Sue) that had never been published before. Like those before her, Bianchi altered the punctuation and capitalization of the poems to make them more agreeable to the reading public. She published *The Single Hound* (1914), *The Life and Letters of Emily Dickinson* (1924), *The Complete Poems of Emily Dickinson* (1924), and *Further Poems of Emily Dickinson* (1929).

Todd and Bianchi continued to publish new editions of the poems throughout the 1930s, each time taking care to include new poems, group the poems by topic, and maintain their standardization. However, the radical rule-breaking in Emily Dickinson's poetry that was so unacceptable to earlier audiences suddenly became highly desirable. Modernism's emphasis on new ways of presenting the fractured nature of life led Thomas Johnson to return to Dickinson's original manuscripts. Determined to undo years of editorializing by various people, Johnson published a three-volume collection, *The Poems of Emily Dickinson*. In this landmark publication, Johnson removes the false titles that earlier editors had written for the poems, restores the irregular capitals and dashes, and numbers the poems in roughly chronological order. Because multiple versions of many poems existed, all with slight variations, Johnson still had to make editorial choices about which words and punctuation marks to include in the "final" versions. However, he kept track of all the variations and published them in a 1955 variorum edition. His 1960 Reading Edition excluded the variations to make the poems easier to read.

Although many editors and critics tackled the problem of Dickinson's publication, Johnson became the gold standard. In 1981, a new landmark editor entered the Dickinson scene. R. W. Franklin decided to build upon and improve Johnson's previous collections of the poems and letters. With each edition of Dickinson's poems or letters, Franklin tried to get closer to representing the original texts. For example, he collected facsimile copies of Dickinson's poems, placed them in their original sequence, and published them as *The Manuscript Books of Emily Dickinson* in 1980. He followed this publication with another breakthrough edition in 1986. Respecting the visual nature of the letters and the importance of spatial relationships on the page, Franklin knew that transcribing the letters into a typewritten format and reformatting them for publication would ruin their natural line breaks. The action would be comparable to taking poems and forcing them into prose. The best way for readers to experience what Dickinson's letters looked like, Franklin reasoned, was to give the public as close a reproduction as possible. So each copy of *The Master Letters of Emily Dickinson* came with an envelope that included a few photographic reproductions of letters, printed onto folded sheets just like the original documents. For many readers, it was as close to holding an original Dickinson letter as they could get.

One of the persistent problems in Dickinson publishing has been how to publish the poems. Should they be organized in quatrains or triplets, as they often were in letters, or as free verse, which she used in the fascicles?[9] Were Dickinson's handwritten line breaks intentional, or did she have to break the line where the page ended? Should line breaks be put where the form dictates, or where Dickinson's hand dictates? With each new publication, Franklin tried to get closer to his vision of Dickinson's original intent.

Perhaps the most complete and faithful edition of Dickinson's poetry is Franklin's three-volume variorum, which he published in 1998. A variorum is a collection that presents all of the known word variations of each poem. If a reader wanted to compare a poem sent to Susan Dickinson, for example, against a version sent to Higginson, Franklin's variorum provides the differences. However, Franklin still had to make several editorial decisions in terms of how the poems would be arranged and presented. In the variorum, poems are listed chronologically and are regularized – they are often presented as eight-line poems divided into two stanzas.

Like the publication of the poems, the publication history of the letters is also marked by confusion and controversy, which led to "the formation of the Dickinson Editing Collective in 1992 . . . currently concentrating on reexamining and problematizing Johnson's and Franklin's print translations of Dickinson's calligraphy, punctuation, lineation, capitalization, and stanza format, as well as developing alternative forms of editing Dickinson's highly unstable texts."[10] Dickinson often drafted multiple versions of letters and changed them slightly to suit the different people they were being sent to. This led to the multiple variations of poems and letters today.

The effects of Dickinson's complex publication history continue, even in modern-day high schools and college classrooms. Should instructors refer to the poems by their Johnson numbers, Franklin numbers, or use the new Franklin variorum, which introduced a dual-numbering system? Because the poems lack titles, the convention has been to refer to them by their first lines or any of the various numbering systems. Recent changes in publication technology, especially the ability to publish images of the document originals on the Internet, continue to update and increase the access readers have to Dickinson's manuscripts.

Early reception

Emily Dickinson's poetry and biography have lent themselves to extensive research and debate ever since the *Springfield Republican* first published "I taste a liquor never brewed" as "The May-Wine" in 1861. Dickinson's work has had a powerful impact on the world. Each year new findings and interpretations provide an important extension of thought in the development of Dickinson scholarship, particularly because of the ambiguity that surrounds both the poetry and the letters. The countless articles and books published each year attest to her literary and social influence in America and the rest of the world. Scholars from many countries including Germany, France, Poland, Denmark, Puerto Rico, and Brazil have contributed to Dickinson studies. Eastern thought has also found great merit in Dickinson's work; Japanese critics have produced many articles and books, while fans founded the Emily Dickinson Society of Japan in the 1980s. Clearly, the voice of a woman from a small town in nineteenth-century New England still resonates loudly around the globe, despite her once public silence.

Readers are fascinated by the myth that is Emily Dickinson – that elusive nineteenth-century Amherst poet whose poetry, letters, and life seem a code that begs to be deciphered. For well over a century, readers have studied the Dickinson canon – one which Helen Hunt Jackson urged Dickinson to publish during her lifetime. Disappointed by Dickinson's refusal to share her poems with the world, Jackson wrote to her: "When you are what men call dead, you will be sorry you were so stingy" (*L* 545, no. 444a). Unfortunately for her contemporaries, only a handful of Dickinson's poems were published during her lifetime.

Before examining the variety of responses to Dickinson's poetry after the widespread publication of her work in the twentieth century, it is helpful to consider her initial reception during the nineteenth century. When critics were first exposed to Dickinson's poetry they had a somewhat gendered reaction:

whereas private readers and female reviewers showed great excitement and appreciation for the poetry, their public, male counterparts felt differently. Arguing over the "likeability" of the poems rather than the deeper elements of style and content, these first critics expanded their more superficial discussions after Thomas Wentworth Higginson and Mabel Loomis Todd edited and published *Poems* (1890, 1891, 1896) and *Letters* (1894). In fact, Higginson was one of the first to extend the discussion to the complexities of Dickinson's poetry. In seeing the irregularity of form and the originality of content as conflicting, he broached a topic that would consume the minds of scholars for years to come.

In considering the effects of Dickinson's publication on nineteenth-century Americans, Marietta Messmer's book *A Vice for Voices* (2001) claims that the demand for Dickinson's poems and biographical information was "intense."[11] Americans found great pride in Dickinson's life and work, a fact that became important for securing her place in American literature when the release of the 1896 volume launched transatlantic debates over the value of her poetry. Attacking Dickinson's work as "uncivilized" because of her poor grammar and non-conventional writing style, nineteenth-century British critics saw her as a rebel – a rebel who represented the unruly values of America. Ironically, American respondents used this criticism as a means of developing greater national pride. Instead of agreeing with the Europeans that Dickinson's work represents incorrigibility and recklessness, they celebrated Dickinson as a symbol of the American ability to think alternatively and creatively.

With the help of two twentieth-century scholastic compilations, academics advanced Dickinson studies by addressing the issue of editing. The first comprehensive edition that highlighted this progress, Willis J. Buckingham's *Emily Dickinson's Reception in the 1890s: A Documentary History* (1989), gave readers 600 articles that provided a breadth of opinions and analysis. As a result, modern-day readers could see the conflicting opinions of the time, while also forming their own opinions about the topics discussed in the various newspapers, journals, and magazines. Klaus Lubbers' *Emily Dickinson: The Critical Revolution* (1968) also proved just as important in developing a foundation for Dickinson studies. Covering all criticism between 1862 and 1962, this book allows readers to track the earlier debates about Dickinson and her work.

Lubbers' book includes a discussion of the 1914 book, *The Single Hound*, written by Dickinson's niece, Martha Dickinson Bianchi. *The Single Hound* became a catalyst for Dickinson studies in the early part of the century. Dickinson's rhyme, meter, and grammar sparked a number of important discussions, many of which centered on the question of editing. *The Single Hound* also provoked readers to question Bianchi's version of events, since her knowledge of Dickinson's "peculiar mind" was based on second-hand accounts rather than eyewitness, verifiable facts. Regardless of Bianchi's own bias, the book helped the public begin to regard Dickinson as one of the best American poets.

New Criticism

Meanwhile, the debate surrounding Dickinson's rhetoric and style continued with great force. In the 1930s, a new critical and analytical approach took hold in Dickinson studies and continued until the late 1950s. This movement, called New Criticism, emphasized the actual words on the page rather than the author's intent. Championed by Allen Tate and Cleanth Brooks, New Criticism urged readers to explore the paradoxes of language and construction of meaning. Because New Critics focused entirely on the works alone, they considered author biography, historical context, and anything outside the works to be irrelevant. Although some critics in the 1950s advocated reading Dickinson's poems in larger contexts (Richard Chase argued that Dickinson should be contextualized as a Puritan ancestor and Rebecca Patterson argued that Dickinson was a lesbian), their opinions were not given any serious thought until much later.

The popularity of New Criticism meant that Dickinson scholars now needed a trustworthy edition of her poetry, one that was true to her handwritten originals. The existing editions were not sufficient because multiple editors had tampered with the poems according to the tastes of their time. For example, Dickinson's first editors were constrained by a reading audience that demanded regular rhyme, traditional meter, and recognizable structure. In an attempt to satisfy these demands, early editors standardized her poems, adding titles, inventing rhymes, and grouping the lines into neat quatrains. Although necessary at the time to sell books, these changes were now viewed as barriers to understanding the real meaning of the poems.

Editor Thomas Johnson set out to fulfill the need for editions of Dickinson's works that were true to the originals. As the first scholar to access both collections of Dickinson's poetry (Amherst College held Susan Dickinson's collection and Harvard University held Millicent Todd Bingham's collection), Johnson could see Dickinson's work in its entirety. He decided to make both sets of papers available to the public and created two volumes that closely adhered to the originals. Although Johnson was forced to make some judgment calls about Dickinson's penmanship, her use of the dash, and the correct order of poems, he nonetheless produced collections of integrity that remained as faithful to

Dickinson's manuscripts as possible. His collections of Dickinson's poems and letters proved to be extraordinarily influential.

More than twenty years later, Ralph W. Franklin contested Johnson's work by arguing that Dickinson's poems were not arranged in chronological order, but according to how they were placed within her bureau. Franklin had the tedious job of scrutinizing stray marks on the various pages and the pinhole pricks on the papers that were sewn into fascicles, in order to determine where each poem was placed in the drawer – he believed this placement determined the date each poem was written. Franklin's work in the past quarter-century reflects the earnest desire of scholars to honor Dickinson's originals when reproducing the poems in book form. His reproduction of the manuscript holographs allows readers to encounter the texts in their handwritten form. In addition to a deeper consideration of Dickinson's syntax and poetics in light of her penmanship, readers gain a different perspective on the poems' organization by seeing them in a context different from Johnson's chronology. Franklin's research has been notable for much more, however, as his three-volume, boxed variorum *Poems of Emily Dickinson* (1998) provides meticulous notes on sources, dates, and alternative versions of the poems. As he and others continue to develop more hypotheses about Dickinson's poetry and life, they work to answer the persistent questions surrounding her work.

With the advent of the technological age, editorial questions are changing because of the increased accessibility of Dickinson's work across the Internet. Although Johnson's and Franklin's efforts have spread across the globe, now nearly all scholars and students have access to Dickinson's manuscripts on the Internet. With the help of hypertext formatting, anyone with a computer can visit a website and interpret the handwriting and marks of punctuation on their own. Critic Martha Nell Smith spearheads these efforts, as does Paul Crumbley in his call for a compromised typographic text that would represent to some degree the variations in punctuation. Lastly, the University of Virginia has created the Emily Dickinson Editing Collective at www.emilydickinson.org, which aims to present Dickinson's writing in its original form, making her idiosyncratic writing more accessible to the wider public.

Editing debates have raged in Dickinson studies over the years, but they share the spotlight with many other scholarly approaches. Issues surrounding Dickinson's biography have been debated steadily since the 1930s, when academics examined all aspects of Dickinson's world for meaning – many interpreting Dickinson's words as a reflection of her nineteenth-century culture. Works by Allen Tate (1932) and George Frisbie Whicher (1938) emphasize more Historicist readings of Dickinson's life and work, opposing the New Critics of their time. During this time period, others presented Dickinson as a descendant of Puritanism and Transcendentalism. In his 1951 biography, Richard Chase traces the importance of Dickinson's New England heritage. Years later, scholars like Jane Donahue Eberwein and Susan Howe argued over the impact of these cultural influences on Dickinson's life and work.

Historicist critics try to gain access to the culture of the mid- to late 1800s by placing Dickinson within important religious and social contexts. Although some Dickinson academics like Elizabeth Shepley Sergeant had been classifying Dickinson as a Transcendentalist since 1914, the focus on both Historicism and Transcendentalism took an even greater hold in the latter part of the century. In his book, *Nimble Believing*, James McIntosh directly connects Dickinson to intellectuals like Thoreau and Melville. By placing her in the ranks of these metaphysical and phenomenological authors, McIntosh explains the invaluable roles each play in shaping the course of American literature.

Likewise, Karl Keller takes a historical approach in *The Only Kangaroo among the Beauty* (1979) by placing Dickinson alongside Anne Bradstreet, Nathaniel Hawthorne, Walt Whitman, and others. The book demonstrates the effects these authors had on the fabric and texture of American culture. For example, Dickinson's letters and poems can be anthropological tools for excavating details about the years between 1830 and 1886. Keller argues that these authors help today's readers understand the genesis and growth of American culture.

Because Transcendentalism and Puritanism revolve predominantly around philosophical concepts, it is no surprise then that the initial discussion of Dickinson in the early 1900s focuses on her metaphysical nature. Because the New Critics had spent most of their efforts considering Dickinson as a wit and a mystic, they had laid a solid foundation for interpreting both her life and her work in a metaphysical context. The philosophical nature of her work and the metaphysical criticism created a variety of responses during the New Critic era, and continued later in the century with critics like Ben Kimpel who examined Dickinson's work as an attempt to express an "ultimate reality" in *Emily Dickinson as Philosopher* (1981).

As scholars approached Dickinson's work with these different perspectives and as New Criticism waned with Johnson's publication of the poems and letters, literary critics began to more fully examine the questions surrounding Emily Dickinson's life. In the highly influential book, *The Years and Hours of Emily Dickinson* (1960), Jay Leyda provides an anti-New Critical biography in chronological order that places Dickinson's nineteenth-century world on the page without any twentieth-century commentary. Following Leyda's work, Richard B. Sewall approaches Dickinson's work with more of a culturally anthropological perspective, paying closer attention to describing and defining the textured details of the time in which she lived. In addition to this perspective, Sewall provides readers with a valuable exploration of Mabel Loomis Todd's love affair with Austin.

The demand for more socially focused biographies extended into the 1980s and 1990s, particularly with the work of Bettina L. Knapp and Barton Levi St Armand. Knapp's comprehensive biography (1986) takes a psychoanalytical approach in considering Dickinson's piety and family background while St Armand aims to provide great texture to Dickinson's world in *Emily Dickinson and Her Culture: The Soul's Society* (1984) by giving a reassessment of nineteenth-century American pop culture and literature.

Sewall's biography, however, proves to be the catalyst for all others and therefore has revolutionized the way readers look at Dickinson and her work. The first wave of feminist scholarship begins with this biography and is extended further with the publication of Adrienne Rich's highly influential essay "Vesuvius at Home: The Power of Emily Dickinson" (1975). Within this piece, Rich asserts Dickinson's awareness of her time and place as expressed in her poetry. Shortly thereafter, Sandra M. Gilbert and Susan Gubar, in *The Madwoman in the Attic: The Woman Writer and the Nineteenth-Century Literary Imagination* (1979), focus on Emily Dickinson's achievement in maneuvering between life and art as a woman in contention with a male-dominated society. Barbara Mossberg builds on these ideas in her own work, largely criticizing the male-created idea of Dickinson as "myth" and corroborating her image as the light-hearted, girlish virgin. Vivian Pollak's *The Anxiety of Gender* (1984) seeks to prove how Dickinson's contemporaries only responded to men's actions within the cultural framework, whereas Dickinson sought to go beyond the identification with this unequal power. In fact, Pollak claims that Dickinson tried to address the gender inequality and pay great attention to the "origins and consequences of her social isolation," and "wished to but could not conceive of female friendships as an effective resolution to her status anxieties."[12]

Other critics compare Dickinson with her contemporaries in order to better understand the gender gap Dickinson overcame in her life and poetry. Joanne Feit Diehl's book, *Dickinson and the Romantic Imagination* (1981) determines that Dickinson is a Romantic who should be critically approached in the same manner as Wordsworth, Shelley, and Keats. Recognizing the risks Dickinson takes in her writing, particularly that of being a female poet in a male-dominated culture, Diehl acknowledges Dickinson's connection to and alienation from the male-dominated Romantic poets. According to Diehl, Dickinson's topics and rhetoric allow her to gain a group identity with the Romantics, but also an individualism that stems from her gendered disconnection from this same group.

Some feminist scholars are not convinced that Dickinson was a highly self-conscious poet who was fully aware of her authorial intention. Instead, they view Dickinson's method and approach to poetry and life as reasonable choices considering her status as an affluent, educated woman living in the nineteenth century. These critics claim Dickinson allied herself with the masculine in order to gain power. Describing Dickinson as a failed feminist, scholars like Cheryl Walker and Joanne Dobson focus on Dickinson's shortfalls in her roles. Many see her as an elusive figure whose privileged lifestyle enabled her to explore her identity as independent, gendered, and social. Dobson articulates this idea in *Dickinson and the Strategies of Reticence* (1989) when she writes that "it was Dickinson who lived out her life to an extreme degree the ethos of ideal womanhood" (55). According to Dobson, it was Dickinson's privileged lifestyle that allowed these poems to be written in the first place.

Some feminist critics also analyze Emily Dickinson's work through her relations with women, while also considering the possibility of the poetry's homoerotic elements. Rather than compare her life and work to the male tradition, feminist critics applaud Dickinson as an exemplar of a woman's capability. For example, Paula Bennett in *Emily Dickinson: Woman Poet* (1990) examines Dickinson's strength as seen in her patterns of erotic imagery, while also expressing a repulsion from men and their power. These ideas take prominence in Marietta Messmer's *A Vice for Voices* (2001) when she argues that Dickinson's poetry is a performative act, "an art that tries to be haunted with the composite workings of an anonymous, universalized mind . . . [one] haunted with the human history of a particular female nature discovering in its encounters with sexual tradition the limits of traditionlessness" (21). Dickinson's unorthodox writing, then, liberates her thoughts while also confining her to the system of linguistic normalcy.

The consideration and interpretation of Dickinson as lesbian has continued to develop since Patterson first postulated this idea in 1951. John Cody's 1971 biography furthers this notion and his psychoanalytical approach to Dickinson's life and work gives greater validity to the argument. Since both these works premiered, many scholars recognize and evaluate the homoerotic elements within Dickinson's work, while also considering the possibility of a lesbian love affair during her lifetime. Martha Nell Smith's work in the early 1990s goes so far as to claim that the "Master" letters may have, in fact, been written to a woman. Clearly the issues of gender and sexuality have impacted the world of Dickinson scholarship, and as a result of this open dialogue, scholars have provided invaluable perspectives on an important and intriguing poet.

Work on Dickinson's rhetoric did not fully develop until after the emergence of feminist criticism. Critics have been unable to agree on the poetic analysis of content and form and, as a result, Dickinson rhetoricians divided into three groups. The first group, led by Helen McNeil, contends that although Dickinson's audience was her very private self, she used her schooling of proper grammar and mechanics to effectively guide her persuasive writing. The second group, however, offers that Dickinson's experimentation with and control of diction, syntax, and voice proved her to be an effective communicator, rather than a confusing, but eloquent one as Dorothy Huff Oberhaus' study of the fascicles claims. The final group has examined Dickinson's work as a series of letters and therefore argues that she simply attempts to persuade her addressees of her opinions and beliefs in her writing. Both Judith Farr and Martha Nell Smith center much of their work on providing the proper background for Dickinson's social sphere in order to best analyze her circumference of correspondence.

The impact of deconstruction, which began in the 1960s, coincided with that of the rhetoricians, and similarly launched a variety of new possibilities for interpretation. Because deconstructive analysis allows for meaning to follow virtually any path, scholarship has expanded greatly over the past twenty years. Not only has deconstruction led to more advanced feminist readings, but it has also allowed Dickinson's poems to be read as allegories of language. Deconstructionists also see the value of Dickinson's use of metonymy, whereas previous critics considered her use of metaphor to be the most important characteristic of her work. In *Dickinson: The Modern Idiom*, David Porter considers the value of her thought and art form: "Dickinson's radical modernism thus is not a theme but a way of knowing, a way of art: it is an idiom of irrepressible consciousness and inescapable derangement come together."[13] Porter's merging of the artistic, linguistic, and psychological aspects is a perfect example of how deconstructionists attempt to discern meaning on the deepest, most complex levels in Emily Dickinson's work.

Dickinson's legacy today

Academic criticism of the past twenty years has blended issues of Dickinson's psychology, biography, history, and, most importantly, linguistics. In analyzing her use of diction and syntax, twentieth-century critics have helped shape Dickinson studies into a field of gigantic proportions. The emphasis placed on Dickinson's writing, mixed with all of these other aspects, has allowed scholars to more fully understand Dickinson's mind and art.

Not only has Dickinson greatly affected the development of important critical viewpoints, but she has also greatly influenced other writers. As observed in *An American Triptych* (1984):

William Carlos Williams, who called Emily Dickinson "his patron saint," acknowledged her influence on his poetry. His concept of the variable foot as a relative, not a fixed, stress, using the breath and inflection of American speech instead of rigid accent and measured syllables to determine phrase and line length, is based on Dickinson's flexible organic metrics. Similarly inspired by Dickinson's poetry are Robert Frost's "sentence sounds" – the rhythms of everyday speech loosely structured by standard poetic forms – and Ezra Pound's "functional," as opposed to "forced," metrics.[14]

In an interesting anecdote noted in Jay Parini's biography of Robert Frost, not only did Dickinson greatly affect Frost's poetry, but she also played an integral role in shaping his biography. Attempting to court his eventual wife, Elinor White, Frost sought to impress her by reading her favorite poems by Sir Philip Sidney and Edmund Spenser, while he introduced White to his own favorite – Emily Dickinson.

The poet Marianne Moore was also greatly influenced by Dickinson's poetry. In *The Anxiety of Gender* (1984), Vivian Pollak writes that Dickinson was an "ally" to Moore in her search for finding the proper voice for articulating her thoughts and emotions: "pointed, yet not sour; powerful, yet not masculinized; moral, yet not didactic."[15] Since the release of the Johnson edition of Dickinson's poetry and letters, many poets have used Dickinson's influence to guide their writing. Poets like Robert Lowell, Theodore Roethke, Allen Ginsberg, Wallace Stevens, and Sylvia Plath all incorporate aspects of Dickinson in their poetry, all the while proclaiming her to be one of the best poets in the world. Adrienne Rich's poem "E" shows the incalculable effects Dickinson has had.[16]

Poets such as Rich, Hart Crane, Joyce Carol Oates, and Billy Collins have admired Dickinson's power and control over her creative life as well as her pioneering use of language. Mimicking the style of Dickinson and pondering the poet's abstruse thought, Crane wrote "To Emily Dickinson":

> You who desired so much – in vain to ask –
> Yet fed your hunger like an endless task,
> Dared dignify the labor, bless the quest –
> Achieved that stillness ultimately best,
>
> Being, of all, least sought for: Emily, hear!
> O sweet, dead Silencer, most suddenly clear
> When singing that Eternity possessed
> And plundered momently in every breast;
>
> – Truly no flower yet withers in your hand.
> The harvest you descried and understand

> Needs more than wit to gather, love to bind.
> Some reconcilement of remotest mind –
> Leaves Ormus rubyless, and Ophir chill.
> Else tears heap all within one clay-cold hill.[17]

Oates' tribute, "Half-Cracked Poetess," highlights the importance of Dickinson while also addressing the many questions she leaves for readers to discern on their own:

> On my finger an antique ring I hadn't
> deserved, but got. Like so much, you're thinking
> meanly, and you'd be right.
> And now the stone is cracked, a tiny disaster,
> the opal's mild fiery light stares out
> and no reflection.
> Like an eye, in a way. Blind
> but still seeing
> except, what is it seeing? –
> and why?[18]

Although poetry is the most obvious creative medium that Dickinson has influenced, she has also had a significant impact on music, theatre, dance, film, art, and popular culture. Some musicians, such as the 1960s' folk group Simon and Garfunkel, have written songs about Dickinson or referenced her in their lyrics. Other musicians, from opera sopranos to rock singers, have sung Dickinson's poems to music. There have also been several successful theatrical productions of different parts of Dickinson's life and her work. Author Susan Glaspell based her 1931 Pulitzer Prize-winning play, *Alison's House*, on Dickinson's life. The most well-known play about Dickinson – William Luce's *The Belle of Amherst* (1976) – was a favorite with critics and audiences alike. The play had great success on Broadway and earned the leading actress, Julie Harris, a Tony Award.

Dance has also incorporated aspects of Dickinson's life and poetry, beginning with Martha Graham's 1940 piece, *Letter to the World*. In this production, Graham focuses on Dickinson's romantic life, creating choreography appropriately matched to her personal relationships and experiences. These experiences are divided into five stages, each using a different poem in its telling of the story. Both Heinz Poll with his *Called Back – Emily* (1984), and Warren Spears with his *Rowing in Eden* (1987), created ballets which sought to depict Dickinson's romantic life and the beauty of her words.

Visual artists honor Dickinson's work in a variety of ways. For example, Joseph Cornell pays homage to Dickinson by creating "box constructions" that include collages, painted interiors, grids, and objects. Roni Horn, Paul Katz, and Lesley Dill have also used Dickinson as inspiration for their art. Dill makes sculptures that incorporate actual words from Dickinson's poems. The wealth of artists inspired by Dickinson led to the first major visual art exhibition devoted to and inspired entirely by Dickinson, organized by Susan Danly at Amherst College's Mead Art Museum in 1997.

Actress Julie Harris, artist Lesley Dill, poet Billy Collins, and critic Polly Longsworth are all featured in Jim Wolpaw's playful 2002 documentary, *Loaded Gun: Life, and Death, and Dickinson –*. This film chronicles one man's quest to understand the woman behind the mythology and to explore what Dickinson means to different types of people. Dickinson's popularity can be experienced to the fullest at the Emily Dickinson Museum in Amherst, Massachusetts, where visitors from around the world go to walk through The Homestead and The Evergreens and attend events such as marathon readings of all of Dickinson's poems.

The expanding wealth of Dickinson art and scholarship allows readers to delve into the mind and works of one of America's finest poets. As readers gain greater access to Dickinson's manuscripts with the help of online resources, interest in her work continues to grow. Practically unknown during her own lifetime, Dickinson is now regarded as one of the most influential poets in American literary history. She is no longer misunderstood as a mousy, reclusive spinster who wrote poetry in her spare time; instead, Emily Dickinson has come to be appreciated as a courageous pioneer of a bold and modern poetic style that commands an international readership.

Notes

1 Life

1. Martha Dickinson Bianchi, *The Life and Letters of Emily Dickinson* (Boston: Houghton Mifflin, 1930), pp. 7–8.
2. Alfred Habegger, *My Wars Are Laid Away in Books: The Life of Emily Dickinson* (New York: Modern Library, 2002), p. 46.
3. Ibid., p. 23.
4. Polly Longsworth, "Edward Dickinson," in *An Emily Dickinson Encyclopedia*, ed. Jane Donahue Eberwein (Westport, CT: Greenwood Press, 1998), pp. 67–70.
5. Jay Leyda, *The Years and Hours of Emily Dickinson*, 2 vols. (New Haven: Yale University Press, 1960), vol. I, p. 3.
6. Ibid., p. 4.
7. Ibid., p. 46.
8. Habegger, *My Wars Are Laid Away*, p. 52.
9. Diana Fuss, *The Sense of an Interior: Four Writers and the Rooms That Shaped Them* (New York: Routledge, 2004), pp. 26–8.
10. Connie Ann Kirk, *Emily Dickinson: A Biography* (Westport, CT: Greenwood Press, 2004), p. 20.
11. Fuss, *Sense of an Interior*, p. 28.
12. Habegger, *My Wars Are Laid Away*, p. 139.
13. Kirk, *Emily Dickinson*, p. 28.
14. Habegger, *My Wars Are Laid Away*, p. 157.
15. Ibid., p. 192.
16. Bianchi, *Life and Letters*, p. 22.
17. Habegger, *My Wars Are Laid Away*, p. 193.
18. Ibid., p. 262.
19. Bianchi, *Life and Letters*, p. 12.
20. Habegger, *My Wars Are Laid Away*, p. 222.
21. Kirk, *Emily Dickinson*, p. 43.
22. Fuss, *Sense of an Interior*, p. 59.
23. Habegger, *My Wars Are Laid Away*, p. 226.
24. Cynthia Griffin Wolff, *Emily Dickinson* (New York: Alfred A. Knopf, 1986), p. 49.
25. Leyda, *Years and Hours*, vol. I, p. 14.

26. Ibid., p. 38.
27. Ibid., p. 44.
28. Bianchi, *Life and Letters*, p. 17.
29. Habegger, *My Wars Are Laid Away*, p. 114.
30. Bianchi, *Life and Letters*, pp. 13–14.
31. Ibid., p. 14.
32. Ibid., p. 219.
33. Wolff, *Emily Dickinson*, p. 7.
34. Bianchi, *Life and Letters*, p. 64.
35. Ibid., p. 67.
36. Habegger, *My Wars Are Laid Away*, p. 353.
37. Ibid.
38. Habegger, *My Wars Are Laid Away*, p. 586.
39. Thomas H. Johnson (ed.), *The Letters of Emily Dickinson* (Cambridge: Harvard University Press, 1986), p. 476.
40. Habegger, *My Wars Are Laid Away*, p. 621.
41. Fuss, *Sense of an Interior*, p. 48.
42. Kirk, *Emily Dickinson*, p. 111.
43. Habegger, *My Wars Are Laid Away*, p. 623.
44. Ibid., p. 111.
45. Kirk, *Emily Dickinson*, pp. 111–12.
46. Barbara Lloyd-Evans (ed.), *The Poems of Emily Bronte* (Savage, MD: Barnes and Noble Books, 1992), p. 71.
47. Fuss, *Sense of an Interior*, p. 69.

2 Context

1. Kirk, *Emily Dickinson*, p. 14.
2. Wolff, *Emily Dickinson*, p. 66.
3. Habegger, *My Wars Are Laid Away*, p. 240.
4. Christopher Benfey, "Emily Dickinson and the American South," in *The Cambridge Companion to Emily Dickinson*, ed. Wendy Martin (Cambridge: Cambridge University Press, 2002), p. 39.
5. Habegger, *My Wars Are Laid Away*, p. 266.
6. Ibid., p. 382.
7. Ibid., p. 373.
8. Ralph Waldo Emerson, *Essays and Poems* (New York: Library of America, 1996), p. 267.
9. Shira Wolosky, "Public and Private in Dickinson's War Poetry," in *A Historical Guide to Emily Dickinson*, ed. Vivian R. Pollak (Oxford: Oxford University Press, 2004), p. 115.
10. Habegger, *My Wars Are Laid Away*, p. 402.

11. Alfred, Lord Tennyson, "The Charge of the Light Brigade," in *The Norton Anthology of English Literature*, vol. II, ed. M. H. Abrams (New York: W. W. Norton & Company, 1993), p. 1133.

3 Works

1. Wendy Martin, *An American Triptych: Anne Bradstreet, Emily Dickinson, Adrienne Rich* (Chapel Hill: University of North Carolina Press, 1984), p. 136.
2. James McIntosh, *Nimble Believing: Dickinson and the Unknown* (Ann Arbor: University of Michigan Press, 2000), p. 17.
3. E. Miller Budick, *Emily Dickinson and the Life of Language: A Study of Symbolic Poetics* (Baton Rouge: Louisiana State University Press, 1985), p. 14.
4. Martin, *American Triptych*, p. 138.
5. Ibid.
6. Selma Bishop, *Isaac Watts, Hymns and Spiritual Songs, 1707–1748: A Study in Early Eighteenth-Century Language Changes* (London: Faith Press, 1962), pp. 236–7.
7. Ibid., p. 56.
8. Martin, *American Triptych*, p. 120.
9. Ibid., p. 137.
10. Judith Farr and Louise Carter, *The Gardens of Emily Dickinson* (Cambridge: Harvard University Press, 2004), p. 26.
11. Ellen Louise Hart and Martha Nell Smith (eds.), *Open Me Carefully: Emily Dickinson's Intimate Letters to Susan Huntington Dickinson* (Ashfield, MA: Paris Press, 1998), pp. xxi–xxii.
12. Martin, *American Triptych*, p. 160.
13. Ibid., p. 113.
14. Habegger, *My Wars Are Laid Away*, p. 232.
15. Kirk, *Emily Dickinson*, p. 80.
16. Habegger, *My Wars Are Laid Away*, p. 441.
17. Martin, *American Triptych*, p. 81.
18. Wolff, *Emily Dickinson*, p. 121.
19. Ibid., p. 120.
20. Habegger, *My Wars Are Laid Away*, p. 360.
21. Coventry Patmore, *The Angel in the House* (London: Macmillan and Co., 1863), p. 83.
22. Ibid., p. 109.
23. Ibid., p. 89.
24. Martin, *American Triptych*, p. 152.
25. Ibid., p. 115.
26. Aife Murray, "A Yankee Poet's Irish Headquarters," *New Hibernia Review* 6 (2002): 9–17.

27. Ibid.
28. Ibid.
29. Fuss, *Sense of an Interior*, p. 35.
30. Murray, "Yankee Poet's Irish Headquarters," 9–17.
31. Luke's version reproduces Matthew's almost word for word until the last verse. Matthew finishes the passage slightly differently: "If ye then, being evil, know how to give good gifts unto your children, how much more shall your Father which is in heaven give *good things* to them that ask him?" (Matthew 7:11, my emphasis). Luke's version suggests that the good gift the believer should be praying for is the Holy Spirit.
32. See, for example, II Samuel 22:2–3: "The Lord is my rock, and my fortress, and my deliverer; The God of my rock; in him will I trust: he is my shield, and the horn of my salvation, my high tower, and my refuge, my savior."
33. Dickinson is obviously drawing on Christ's parable in which he compares those who hear his "sayings" and obey them to a man who builds his house on a rock which is able to withstand the storm and flood (Matthew 7:24–7). Dickinson is also referencing the famous hymn "Rock of Ages," written in 1776 by Augustus Toplady, which picks up on the image of Christ as the believer's rock. The hymn begins and ends with the lines: "Rock of ages, cleft for me, / Let me hide myself in thee."
34. The corresponding passage in Luke reads slightly differently: "Are not five sparrows sold for two farthings, and not one of them is forgotten before God?" (Luke 12:6).
35. Dickinson was passionate about her relationships with both men and women and used highly charged language to convey the depth of her emotions. This commitment to emotional intimacy in friendship was not unusual in Victorian America. For a discussion about the deep bonds of intimacy expressed in same-sex friendships, especially in Victorian America, see Stephanie Coontz, *Marriage, A History: From Obedience to Intimacy, or How Love Conquered Marriage* (New York: Penguin, 2005).
36. Martin, *American Triptych*, p. 148.
37. In 1853, Emily Dickinson wrote to Austin, "Father takes great delight in your remarks to him – puts on his spectacles and read them o'er and o'er as if it was a blessing to have an only son. He reads all the letters you write as soon as he gets, at the post office, no matter to whom addressed" (*L* 231, no. 108).
38. Martin, *American Triptych*, p. 95
39. While the dating for the letters is conjectural, both Johnson and Franklin place the dates of these letters between these years. The dates I use here depend on Johnson's dating in his *Letters of Emily Dickinson*. For Franklin's dates, see R. W. Franklin (ed.), *The Poems of Emily Dickinson* (Cambridge: Belknap Press, 2003).
40. Ruth Owen Jones, "Neighbor – and Friend – and Bridegroom," *Emily Dickinson Journal* 11 (2002): 48–85.

41. See Adrienne Rich, "Vesuvius at Home: The Power of Emily Dickinson," *Parnassus: Poetry in Review* 5.1 (1976): 49–74, and Joanne Feit Diehl, "'Come Slowly – Eden': The Woman Poet and Her Muse," in *Dickinson and the Romantic Imagination* (Princeton: Princeton University Press, 1981), pp. 13–33.
42. Martin, *American Triptych*, p. 100.
43. Ibid.
44. Ibid.
45. I have eliminated Johnson's alternate readings from the text of Dickinson's "Master" letters in order to preserve continuity.
46. Martin, *American Triptych*, p. 101.
47. Ibid., p. 102.
48. Ibid., p. 103.
49. Calvary was the hill on which Christ was crucified, and thus is a place of sacrifice, suffering, pain, and death. Of course, Christ's resurrection signals a victory over death and suffering – a resurrection and victory that Dickinson seems to be claiming for herself as well.
50. Martin, *American Triptych*, p. 103.
51. *P* 644, no. 1544.
52. Martin, *American Triptych*, p. 127.
53. Ibid., p. 128.
54. Dickinson here is picking up on Christ's admonition to his disciples: "Suffer little children, and forbid them not, to come unto me: for of such is the kingdom of heaven" (Matthew 19:14).
55. See I Corinthians 11:26: "For as often as ye eat this bread, and drink this cup, ye do shew the Lord's death *till he come*" (my emphasis).
56. Walt Whitman's "A Noiseless Patient Spider" is an example of the Transcendentalists' use of nature as a metaphor for the poet:

> A noiseless patient spider,
> I mark'd where on a little promontory it stood isolated,
> Mark'd how to explore the vacant vast surrounding,
> It launched forth filament, filament, filament, out of itself,
> Ever unreeling down, ever tirelessly speeding them.
>
> And you O my soul where you stand,
> Surrounded, detached, in measureless oceans of space,
> Ceaselessly musing, venturing, throwing, seeking the spheres to connect them,
> Till the bridge you will need be form'd, till the ductile anchor hold,
> Till the gossamer thread you fling catch somewhere, O my soul.

Notice how the male-centered Whitman finds the spider useful only in describing himself. Dickinson's interest in the spider is quite different. See Walt Whitman, *Leaves of Grass* (Philadelphia: David McKay, 1891–2), p. 343; see also my analysis of these spider poems in Martin, *American Triptych*, pp. 132–3.
57. Martin, *American Triptych*, p. 123.

58. Ibid., p. 121.
59. Ibid., p. 120. See "A Bee his burnished Carriage" (*P* 579, no. 1339), which describes the bee's ravishment of the unsuspecting flower, and *L* 210, no. 93.
60. Martin, *American Triptych*, p. 146.
61. Ibid.
62. Clarence L. Gohdes, "Emily Dickinson's Blue Fly," *New England Quarterly* 51 (1978): 423.
63. Ibid., 423–4.
64. Janet W. Buell, "'A Slow Solace': Emily Dickinson and Consolation," *New England Quarterly* 62 (1989): 324. According to Buell's calculation, 614 of the 1046 letters in Johnson's edition are from the final decade of Dickinson's life. Of course, this calculation depends on Johnson's dating.
65. Ibid., 334.
66. Ibid., 331–2.
67. Ibid., 329.
68. Barton Levi St Armand, *Emily Dickinson and Her Culture: The Soul's Society* (Cambridge: Cambridge University Press, 1984), p. 59.
69. Maria Magdalena Farland, "'That Tritest/Brightest Truth': Emily Dickinson's Anti-Sentimentality," *Nineteenth-Century Literature* 53 (1998): 370.
70. Ibid., 371.
71. Ibid. Examples of such narratives include *The Last Leaf from Sunny Side* and *The Gates Ajar*, both of which Emily Dickinson apparently read.
72. Farland, "'That Tritest/Brightest Truth,'" 373–4. My interpretation of this poem both draws from and coincides with Farland's similar interpretation.
73. Martin, *American Triptych*, p. 123.
74. Other poems that describe or contemplate the silence of the grave include poem nos. 50, 56, 89, 216, 449, 1065, etc.
75. Martin, *American Triptych*, 142.

4 Reception

1. Martin, *American Triptych*, p. 116.
2. Hart and Smith (eds.), *Open Me Carefully*, p. xxvii.
3. Martin, *American Triptych*, p. 82.
4. Ibid.
5. Habegger, *My Wars Are Laid Away*, p. 526.
6. "Fascicle," *Compact Oxford English Dictionary*. 2nd edn, 1999, p. 570.
7. Martin, *American Triptych*, p. 144.
8. Habegger, *My Wars Are Laid Away*, p. 628.
9. Farr and Carter, *The Gardens of Emily Dickinson*, p. 33.
10. Marietta Messmer, *A Vice for Voices: Reading Emily Dickinson's Correspondence* (Amherst: University of Massachusetts Press, 2001), p. 55.

11. Ibid., p. 4.
12. Vivian Pollak, *Dickinson: The Anxiety of Gender* (Ithaca: Cornell University Press, 1984), p. 30.
13. David Porter, *Dickinson: The Modern Idiom* (Cambridge: Harvard University Press, 1981), p. 6.
14. Martin, *American Triptych*, p. 140.
15. Pollak, *Anxiety of Gender*, p. 336.
16. Adrienne Rich, "E," in *Readings on Emily Dickinson*, ed. Tamara Johnson (San Diego: Greenhaven Press, 1997), p. 37.
17. Hart Crane, "To Emily Dickinson," in *Visiting Emily: Poems Inspired by the Life and Work of Emily Dickinson*, eds. Sheila Coghill and Thom Tammaro (Iowa City: University of Iowa Press, 2000), p. 16.
18. Joyce Carol Oates, "Half-Cracked Poetess," in ibid., p. 72.

Guide to further reading

Note: These books are useful tools to learn more about Emily Dickinson and her works.

Bianchi, Martha Dickinson, *The Life and Letters of Emily Dickinson*, Boston: Houghton Mifflin Company, 1930.
Written by Emily Dickinson's niece (daughter of Austin and Susan), this is a rare first-person account of Dickinson.

Bloom, Harold (ed.), *Modern Critical Views: Emily Dickinson*, New York: Chelsea House Publishers, 1985.
Bloom collects important essays that explore Dickinson's male-dominated society, continuance of Puritan tradition, and reliance on nature.

Cady, Edwin H. and Louis J. Budd (eds.), *On Dickinson: The Best From American Literature*, Durham: Duke University Press, 1990.
A collection of essays that provides a number of interesting interpretations of Dickinson, including Dorothy Huff Oberhaus' analysis of Christ's auspicious role in the poetry.

Eberwein, Jane Donahue (ed.), *An Emily Dickinson Encyclopedia*, Westport, CT: Greenwood Press, 1998.
By far the most accessible and complete resource for fast facts about Dickinson.

Eberwein, Jane Donahue, *Dickinson: Strategies of Limitation*, Amherst: University of Massachusetts Press, 1985.
Eberwein considers the multiple roles Dickinson plays in her poems.

Farr, Judith and Louise Carter, *The Gardens of Emily Dickinson*, Cambridge: Harvard University Press, 2004.
A great resource for learning about the symbolic and personal meanings of flowers in Dickinson's poetry.

Franklin, Ralph William, *The Editing of Emily Dickinson: A Reconsideration*, Madison: University of Wisconsin Press, 1967.
A synopsis of the editorial problems associated with the publication of Dickinson's poems from 1886 through the 1960s.

Fuss, Diana, *The Sense of an Interior: Four Writers and the Rooms That Shaped Them*, New York: Routledge, 2004.
Wonderful re-creation of Dickinson's room and home, along with chapters about Sigmund Freud, Helen Keller, and Marcel Proust.

Gilbert, Sandra M. and Susan Gubar, *The Madwoman in the Attic: The Woman Writer and the Nineteenth-Century Literary Imagination*, New Haven: Yale University Press, 1979.
This groundbreaking work of feminist criticism celebrates Dickinson's achievements in her life and art.

Grabher, Gudrun, Roland Hagenbuchle, and Cristanne Miller (eds.), *The Emily Dickinson Handbook*, Amherst: University of Massachusetts Press, 1998.
This collection by leading critics provides the basics of Dickinson scholarship.

Habegger, Alfred, *My Wars Are Laid Away in Books: The Life of Emily Dickinson*, New York: Modern Library, 2002.
Fascinating biography full of rich details.

Hart, Ellen Louise and Martha Nell Smith (eds.), *Open Me Carefully: Emily Dickinson's Intimate Letters to Susan Huntington Dickinson*, Ashfield, MA: Paris Press, 1998.
This collection reveals Dickinson's closest female relationship, which has historically been censored, suppressed, or neglected by critics.

Heginbotham, Eleanor Elson, *Reading the Fascicles of Emily Dickinson: Dwelling in Possibilities*, Columbus: Ohio State University Press, 2003.
Heginbotham examines four fascicles in Dickinson's collection.

Johnson, Thomas (ed.), *The Complete Poems of Emily Dickinson*, Boston: Little, Brown and Company, University Press, 1960.
The first single-volume collection of all of the poems and a gold standard in Dickinson scholarship.

Johnson, Thomas, *Emily Dickinson: An Interpretive Biography*, Cambridge: Harvard University Press, 1955.
Written by one of the most important Dickinson scholars, this book investigates the traditions and people of Dickinson's life, the interests and motivations of her mind, and finally, the poetry itself.

Johnson, Thomas H. (ed.), *Emily Dickinson: Selected Letters*, Cambridge: Belknap Press of Harvard University, 1986.
A solid collection that introduces the reader to Dickinson's letters, relationships, and character.

Johnson, Thomas (ed.), *The Poems of Emily Dickinson*, 3 vols., Cambridge: Harvard University Press, 1951.
A monumental collection: Johnson analyzes penmanship and punctuation in order to honor Dickinson's original handwritten copies.

Juhasz, Suzanne (ed.), *Feminist Critics Read Emily Dickinson*, Bloomington: Indiana University Press, 1983.
The essays focus on Dickinson's exploration of power as she considers control and possibilities in the world.

Juhasz, Suzanne, *The Undiscovered Continent: Emily Dickinson and the Space of the Mind*, Bloomington: Indiana University Press, 1983.
Explores Dickinson as a powerful mind that overcame the pressures of a male-dominated society.

Juhasz, Suzanne and Cristanne Miller (eds.), *Emily Dickinson: A Celebration for Readers*, New York: Gordon and Breach, 1989.
A comprehensive collection of essays by scholars, focusing on topics such as the dualism in Dickinson's poetry.

Keller, Karl, *The Only Kangaroo among the Beauty: Emily Dickinson and America*, Baltimore: Johns Hopkins University Press, 1979.
This influential work places Dickinson within the early American contexts of Puritanism and Transcendentalism.

Leyda, Jay, *The Years and Hours of Emily Dickinson*, 2 vols., New Haven: Yale University Press, 1960.
By using her letters, Leyda creates a valuable time-line for understanding Dickinson's life and relationships, as well as the society in which she lived.

Longsworth, Polly, *Austin and Mabel: The Amherst Affair and Love Letters of Austin Dickinson and Mabel Loomis Todd*, New York: Farrar, Straus and Giroux, 1983.
This collection provides valuable insight into the passionate love affair that affected the eventual editing and publication of Dickinson's work.

Loving, Jerome, *Emily Dickinson: The Poet on the Second Story*, New York: Cambridge University Press, 1986.
Loving analyzes Dickinson's words, images, and the "Master" letters to help the reader understand the paradoxes in her writing.

Lubbers, Klaus, *Emily Dickinson: The Critical Revolution*, Ann Arbor: University of Michigan Press, 1968.
Essential for all scholars studying the history of Dickinson criticism, this book traces the earlier academic approaches to Dickinson's work.

Martin, Wendy, *An American Triptych*, Chapel Hill: University of North Carolina Press, 1984.
A careful study of Anne Bradstreet, Emily Dickinson, and Adrienne Rich: three inter-connected American women poets from three different eras.

Martin, Wendy (ed.), *The Cambridge Companion to Emily Dickinson*, Cambridge: Cambridge University Press, 2002.
Essays by international Dickinson scholars that place her work in the contexts of literature, culture, and politics.

Messmer, Marietta, *A Vice for Voices: Reading Emily Dickinson's Correspondence*, Amherst: University of Massachusetts Press, 2001.

Messmer scrutinizes Dickinson's letters, providing their publishing history, reception, and publication controversies.

Miller, Cristanne, *Emily Dickinson: A Poet's Grammar*, Cambridge: Harvard University Press, 1987.

Miller focuses on the language, punctuation, and peculiar gaps of meaning in Dickinson's work.

Pollak, Vivian R., *A Poet's Parents: The Courtship Letters of Emily Norcross and Edward Dickinson*, Chapel Hill: University of North Carolina Press, 1988.

This is an interesting collection of letters that shows the early correspondence between Emily Dickinson's parents. Pollack then links emotions reflected in the letters to Dickinson's work.

St Armand, Barton Levi, *Emily Dickinson and Her Culture: The Soul's Society*, Cambridge: Cambridge University Press, 1984.

An important and helpful book that places Dickinson's views about nature, romance, death, and the afterlife within the cultural context.

Sewall, Richard B., *The Life of Emily Dickinson*, 2 vols., New York: Farrar, Straus and Giroux, 1974.

A rich biography with analyses of primary sources that provide multiple perspectives and insight.

Smith, Robert McClure, *The Seductions of Emily Dickinson*, Tuscaloosa: University of Alabama Press, 1996.

A well-detailed discussion of the importance of using an antebellum lens to view the world of Dickinson and examine her texts.

Stocks, Kenneth, *Emily Dickinson and the Modern Consciousness: A Poet of Our Time*, New York: St Martin's Press, 1988.

This book examines Dickinson as a predecessor to Modernism.

Weisbuch, Robert, *Emily Dickinson's Poetry*, Chicago: University of Chicago Press, 1972.

Weisbuch examines Dickinson's work as a product of three major influences – her family upbringing in New England, her ancestral ties to Puritanism, and her connection to powerful writers of the time.

Whicher, George Frisbie, *This Was a Poet: A Critical Biography of Emily Dickinson*, New York: Charles Scribner's Sons, 1938.

This book contextualizes and analyzes the poetry as a reflection of Dickinson's nineteenth-century New England life.

Wolff, Cynthia Griffin, *Emily Dickinson*, New York: Alfred A. Knopf, 1986.

One of the best biographies of Dickinson.

Wolosky, Shira, *Emily Dickinson: A Voice of War*, New Haven: Yale University Press, 1984.
Wolosky concludes that Dickinson's voice contends with those strident voices of her society and that she meditates and then uses language as a means of expressing the conflicts of her physical and metaphysical worlds.

Index

Abolition 14, 30–2
  see also Civil War
Amherst 2, 6, 7, 9, 25, 26, 31, 35, 60,
  71, 79, 85, 87
  The Emily Dickinson Museum,
  Amherst 131
Amherst Academy 5, 7, 8
Amherst College 2, 34, 79, 85, 112, 123,
  131
Atlantic Monthly 14, 20

Bianchi, Martha Dickinson (niece) 18,
  23, 139
  personal recollections 3, 12, 13, 17
  role in ED's publication 118–19
  The Single Hound 122–3
Bible 26, 55, 58–70
  see also religion
Bowles, Samuel 14, 15, 21, 29, 31, 48,
  79, 80, 83, 85, 86, 98
  as editor of ED's poetry 114–15
  see also Dickinson, Emily: letters
Brontë, Charlotte 10–11
Brontë, Emily 23

Calvinism 25, 26
Civil War 18, 24, 25, 26, 29–30, 32,
  34–9
  see also Abolition
Congregationalism 25–6

death 97–109
  ED's own death and funeral 22–3,
  53, 58

of friends 48–9, 97, 98–9
  role in nature 97
Dickinson, Austin (William Austin,
  brother) 3, 4, 7, 12, 13, 14, 17,
  18, 21, 22, 24, 29, 32, 34, 48, 52,
  58, 79, 85, 87, 100
  marriage 15, 53
  relationship with ED 7, 8, 9–10,
  64–5, 77
  relationship with Mabel Loomis
  Todd 21, 22, 119, 126
  see also Dickinson, Emily: letters
Dickinson, Edward (father) 2, 3–4, 5,
  11, 12, 13, 14, 17, 18, 19, 21, 26,
  27, 29, 31, 34, 52, 77, 78, 83, 85,
  87, 98, 105
  marriage 3–4
  relationship with ED 9, 10, 11–13,
  19, 56, 75, 77
  views of women's roles 3, 52, 53
Dickinson, Emily
  fascicles 18, 111, 118
  health problems 9, 21, 22, 98, 117
  "Master" 15, 38
  publication
    feelings about 47, 51, 111, 113,
    115–16
    history 22, 51, 110, 111–22
  punctuation 117–18
    capitalization 111, 112–13,
    117–18
    dashes 41, 117, 118
  seclusion 19–20, 21, 22, 41
  white 18–19, 20, 22

works
  letters 24–5, 31, 33, 34–5, 36,
    47–51: to Bowdoin, Elbridge G.
    10; to Bowles, Mrs Samuel 87;
    to Bowles, Samuel 100; to
    Clark, Charles 98–9; to Cowan,
    Perez 58; to Dickinson, Austin
    7, 8, 10, 11–12, 48, 64–5, 77, 87;
    to Dickinson, Susan Gilbert 50,
    63–4, 71–2, 73, 74–5, 76, 80,
    85, 105–6; to Hale, Edward
    Everett 14; to Higginson,
    Thomas Wentworth 9, 12,
    14–15, 19, 21, 49–50, 62, 75, 77,
    78, 82, 85–6, 105, 113, 115; to
    the Hollands, Dr and Mrs 62,
    63, 68, 83, 86, 87, 99, 100,
    105–6; to Humphrey, Jane 47,
    98; to Lord, Judge Otis 82,
    85–6; to "Master" 77, 78–83; to
    Norcross cousins, Louise and
    Frances 23, 64; to Norcross,
    Joel 65; to Root, Abiah 1, 2,
    5–6, 7, 8, 9, 11, 12, 52,
    54, 55, 60–1, 63, 66, 72–3; to
    Sweetser, Mrs Joseph A.
    70; to Whitney, Maria 48–9,
    65
  poems: "The Admirations – and
    Contempts – of time –" 108;
    "After great pain, a formal
    feeling comes –" 106; "Awake
    ye muses nine, sing me a strain
    divine" 112; "Because I could
    not stop for Death" 101–2;
    "The Beggar at the Door for
    Fame" 56; "The Bible is an
    antique Volume –" 59; "The
    Blunder is in estimate" 108;
    "Death is a supple Suitor" 102;
    "Dust is the only Secret –" 103;
    "Eden is that old-fashioned
    House" 68; "The Fact that
    Earth is Heaven –" 68, 87;
    "Forever is composed of Nows"
    46; "The Gentian weaves her

fringes –" 68; "He forgot – and
    I – remembered –" 65;
    "'Heaven' has different Signs –
    to me –" 68–9; "'Heaven' – is
    what I cannot reach! –" 68;
    "'Hope' is the thing with
    feathers –" 56–7; "How dare
    the robins sing" 106–7; "How
    the old Mountains drip with
    Sunset" 89–90; "I am afraid to
    own a Body –" 46, 117; "I
    cannot live with You –" 65–6;
    "I can't tell you – but you feel
    it –" 68; "I felt a Funeral, in my
    Brain" 103–4; "I have a Bird in
    spring" 98; "I heard a Fly buzz –
    when I died –" 102–3; "I meant
    to have but modest needs –"
    61; "I never felt at Home –
    Below –" 68; "I stepped from
    Plank to Plank" 44; "I taste a
    liquor never brewed –" 112–13,
    121; "I think just how my shape
    will rise –" 67; "I took one
    Draught of Life –" 108; "If I'm
    lost – now" 41–2, 61; "If the
    foolish, call them '*flowers*' –"
    59; "I'll tell you how the Sun
    rose" 15, 50; "I'm ceded – I've
    stopped being Theirs –" 79, 83,
    84–5; "I'm Nobody! Who are
    you?" 116–17; "Is it true, dear
    Sue?" 19; "It feels a shame to be
    Alive –" 35–6, 66; "Mama never
    forgets her birds" 67; "The
    Murmur of a Bee" 90–1; "The
    murmuring of Bees, has
    ceased" 68; "My life closed
    twice before its close –" 107;
    "My Life had stood – a Loaded
    Gun –" 37–8; "My Wars are laid
    away in Books" 39; "Myself can
    read the Telegrams" 28; "A
    narrow Fellow in the Grass"
    113–15, 116; "'Nature' is
    what we see –" 70, 93;

Dickinson, Emily (*cont.*)
  "Nature – sometimes sears a
  Sapling –" 96; "Nature – the
  Gentlest Mother is" 87–8; "The
  nearest Dream recedes
  unrealized" 15, 50; "On this
  wondrous sea" 98; "One need
  not be a Chamber – to be
  Haunted –" 45; "One Sister
  have I in our house" 15–16;
  "Papa above!" 67; "Paradise is
  of the option" 68; "Publication
  – is the Auction" 115–16, 117;
  "'Red Sea' indeed! Talk not to
  me" 43; "Safe in their Alabaster
  Chambers" 15, 50–1; "She
  sweeps with many-colored
  Brooms –" 57; "Sic transit
  Gloria mundi" 112; "The Sky is
  low – the Clouds are mean" 96;
  "Some keep the Sabbath going
  to Church –" 58, 92–3; "Some,
  too fragile for winter winds"
  67; "The Soul selects her own
  Society –" 19–20; "'Sown in
  dishonor'!" 67; "The Spider
  holds a Silver Ball" 93–4;
  "Success is counted sweetest"
  36–7, 115; "The Sun went down
  – no Man looked on –" 94–5,
  96; "There's a certain Slant of
  light" 95–6; "There's the Battle
  of Burgoyne –" 38; "These are
  the days when Birds come back
  –" 56, 68, 91–2; "These are the
  Signs to Nature's Inns –" 56;
  "This Consciousness that is
  aware" 107; "This World is not
  Conclusion" 104–5; "Those –
  dying then" 62; "Title divine –
  is mine!" 79, 83; "To be alive –
  is Power –" 45–6, 109; "To my
  small Hearth His fire came –"
  55; "To own a Susan of my
  own" 75; "Under the Light, yet
  under" 105–6; "Victory comes
  late –" 67; "We play at Paste"
  15, 50; "What Inn is this" 55;
  "What is – 'Paradise' –" 61;
  "When a Lover is a Beggar" 56;
  "When Bells stop ringing –
  Church – begins –" 34; "While
  we were fearing it, it came –"
  29; "Who has not found the
  Heaven – below –" 43–4, 70;
  "Why should we hurry – why
  indeed?" 105; "The Wind
  begun to rock and Grass" 21;
  "The wind drew off" 97; "You
  love me – you are sure –" 74;
  "You're right – 'the way *is*
  narrow' –" 60
Dickinson, Emily Norcross (mother) 4,
    21
  illness 11, 52, 98
  marriage 3–4
Dickinson, Gib (Thomas Gilbert,
    nephew) 18, 21
  death 98, 105–6
Dickinson, Lavinia Norcross (Vinnie,
    sister) 4, 10, 12, 13, 16, 20, 22,
    23, 26, 52, 54, 110, 123
  relationship with her ED 13, 71
  role in publication 117, 118
Dickinson, Ned (Edward, nephew)
    17–18
Dickinson, Samuel (grandfather) 2, 4
Dickinson, Susan Huntington Gilbert
    (Sue, sister-in-law) 14, 20, 21,
    22, 23, 24, 29, 31, 32, 48, 87,
    111, 120, 123
  criticism of ED's poetry 50–1
  marriage to Austin 53
  relationship with ED 15–18, 63–4,
    71–2, 73, 74–5
  role in ED's publication 117, 118–19
  see also Dickinson, Emily: letters
domestic realm 51–2, 58
  the "Angel in the House" 53
  ED's appreciation of 51

the home as church/God 58
as a place to write 52, 55, 77, 78–83
servants 54–5, 87
as a theme in ED's poetry 55, 57
a woman's responsibilities in 51–2,
    54, 58

Edwards, Jonathan 25
Eliot, George 10, 11, 98
Emerson, Ralph Waldo 32–3, 34, 41,
    98, 115, 116
  Poems 14
Evergreens, The 11, 13, 15, 19, 21, 22,
    29, 31, 32, 48, 131

Franklin, Ralph W. 18, 119–21, 124,
    139

Higginson, Thomas Wentworth 14–15,
    21, 23, 31, 33, 34, 36, 40, 49–50,
    51, 57, 62, 77, 78, 79, 83, 84–5,
    86, 113, 115, 120
  his letters about ED 20–1, 40, 57,
    109
  role in ED's publication 117, 118,
    122
  see also Dickinson, Emily: letters
Holland, Dr J. G. and Elizabeth 71
  see also Dickinson, Emily: letters
Homestead, The 4–5, 11, 13, 19, 21, 22,
    23, 58, 59, 131
Humphrey, Jane 71, 73
  see also Dickinson, Emily: letters

industrialism 27–8, 32, 51, 54, 87

Jackson, Helen Hunt 5, 21, 31, 98, 115
  letters to ED 115, 121
  see also Dickinson, Emily: letters
Johnson, Thomas H. 18, 119–20, 121,
    123–4, 129, 140

Lord, Judge Otis Phillips 19, 21, 82,
    85–6, 98, 100
  see also Dickinson, Emily: letters

"Master" 77, 78–83, 85, 86
  see also Dickinson, Emily: letters
Mount Holyoke Female Seminary 8–9,
    11, 60

nature 86–97
  flowers 6–7
  garden 7, 86, 87
  herbarium 6–7
Newton, Benjamin Franklin 14, 15
Norcross, Emily Lavinia (cousin) 8,
    9
Norcross, Louise and Frances
    (Norcross cousins) 23, 34, 71,
    87
  see also Dickinson, Emily: letters

Patmore, Coventry 53
Puritanism 25, 26, 27, 32, 33, 86, 87,
    88, 99, 123, 125

reception, critical 121–31
  deconstruction 128
  feminism 126–7
  historicism 124–5
  Modernism 119
  New Criticism 123, 124, 125
religion 56–7, 58
  ED and faith 52, 58
  Great Awakening 25, 30
  the home as church 58
  light of God 55
  revivals 25, 26, 58, 60
  as theme in ED's poetry and letters
    55
  see also Bible, Calvinism,
    Congregationalism,
    Puritanism, Unitarianism
Root, Abiah 1, 5, 6, 7, 11, 12, 55, 67, 71,
    72–3
  see also Dickinson, Emily: letters

Springfield Republican 14, 51, 112, 113,
    121
Stearns, Lieutenant Frazar 34, 36

Thoreau, Henry David 32, 34
Todd, Mabel Loomis
    relationship with Austin Dickinson
        21–2, 126
    role in ED's publication 22, 117,
        118–19, 122
Transcendentalism 32–4, 86, 93, 115,
    125

Unitarianism 14, 32–6

Victorianism 19, 41, 42, 51, 54, 94, 97,
    98, 103

Wadsworth, Reverend Charles 14, 15,
    21, 29, 79, 83, 98
Watts, Isaac 42–4
Whitman, Walt 32, 34, 48, 116,
    125
women's rights 14, 24,
    31–2